The Church's Response
To
COVID-19

Editors

Robert A. Danielson

Greg S. Whyte

First Fruits Press
Wilmore, Kentucky
c2021

ISBN: **9781648170355**
The Church's response to Covid 19
Robert A. Danielson and Greg S. Whyte editors.
First Fruits Press, ©2021

Digital version at http://place.asburyseminary.edu/firstfruitsheritagematerial/...

For all other uses, contact:
First Fruits Press
B.L. Fisher Library
Asbury Theological Seminary
204 N. Lexington Ave.
Wilmore, KY 40390
http://place.asburyseminary.edu/firstfruits

The Church's response to Covid 19 / editors, Robert A. Danielson and Greg S. Whyte. – Wilmore, Kentucky : First Fruits Press, 2021.

227 pages ; cm.

ISBN: 9781648170355 (paperback)
ISBN: 9781648170362 (uPDF)
ISBN: 9781648170379 (Mobi)
OCLC: 1249448414

1. COVID-19 (Disease)--Religious aspects--Christianity. 2. Epidemics--Religious aspects--Christianity. 3. Diseases--Religious aspects--Christianity. 4. Suffering--Religious aspects--Christianity.
I. Danielson, Robert A. (Robert Alden), 1969- II. Whyte, Greg S., 1980 -

BT162.D57 C58 2021 261.8/321962414

Cover design by Amanda Kessinger

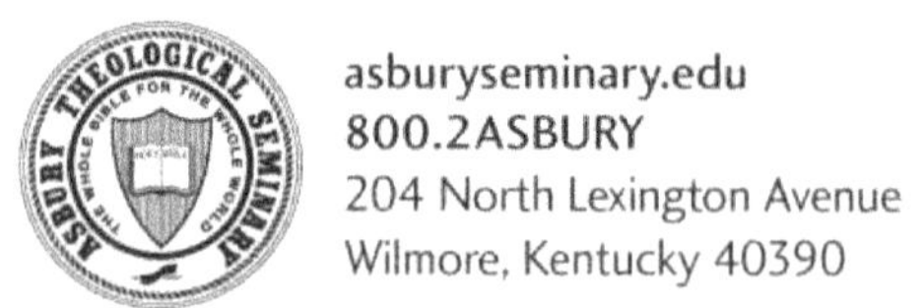

First Fruits Press
The Academic Open Press of Asbury Theological Seminary
204 N. Lexington Ave., Wilmore, KY 40390
859-858-2236
first.fruits@asburyseminary.edu
asbury.to/firstfruits

Table of Contents

Introduction

Robert A. Danielson

As of January 5, 2021, the COVID-19 virus has wreaked havoc on the physical and emotional well-being of the people all over the globe. As of this date, there have been 282,000 total cases in Kentucky with 3,067 total deaths. In the United States there have been 20,900,000 total cases with 354,000 death, and in the entire world there have been 85,900,000 total cases with 1,860,000 deaths. While several vaccines have been created and are currently in the process of distribution, the world is still in the midst of this challenging crisis, a crisis which can only be compared to the Spanish Influenza outbreak of 1919, long before most of us were even born. It is expected that these numbers will rise before they begin to decline.

As a professor at Asbury Theological Seminary in Wilmore, Kentucky, I, like many others, was thrown into the challenge of moving classes online for most of 2020. This was a particular challenge, since I was teaching two courses of Missional Formation, one in the Summer of 2020 and one in the Fall of 2020. This course has traditionally used an ethnographic component to teach students how to study a congregation through observation and interviews, but as churches moved online with social distancing and mask wearing increasing, I was left trying to figure out how to deal with this assignment in an online format.

In the start of this crisis, I was invited to work with two other colleagues on writing a paper on how the Spanish Influenza epidemic impacted Christian Mission.[1] This was an historical approach beginning to wrestle with what impacts COVID-19 might have on Christian mission in the near future. As I delved into my research and writing,

[1] See Robert A. Danielson, Benjamin L. Hartley, and James R. Krabill, "COVID-19 in missiological and historical perspective." *Missiology: An International Review* 49 (1):1-15 (January 2021). DOI: 10.1177/0091829620972386

I realized that very little had been written about the Church's response to the Spanish Influenza epidemic. There were very few accounts about Church work in particular. It was clear that they closed churches in 1919, wore masks, held funerals in people's homes, etc., but the individual accounts of these churches are few and far between. As this reality struck home, I began to develop a thought. What if my students and I embarked on a project to record the Church's response to COVID-19 right now, in the middle of the epidemic? Without knowing the end of the story, we could record exactly what pastors and congregations were thinking in the midst of the crisis. This could be a potential tool for future historians to look back on, as well as a reflective project for the students as well. I decided to craft the assignment to be as specific as possible, and still allow for the creativity of the student writers. The congregations, their pastors, and the lay people interviewed were all to be given pseudonyms by the students, so that even I am unaware of which congregations are involved. However, I asked that, as much as possible, the students keep true to the geographical area and denominational affiliation of churches involved. The best essays, six from the summer and seven from the Fall, are included here. They are kept separate based on which course they took, since the first set of papers reflects the situation as it existed through August of 2020 and the second set demonstrates the situation as of December 2020, and each has its own unique dynamic given the changing context of 2020.

The Kentucky Context

On January 9, 2020, the World Health Organization first announced a mysterious virus from Wuhan, in the People's Republic of China, with pneumonia-like symptoms. On January 21, 2020, the first confirmed case in the United States was identified in Washington State from someone who had returned from Wuhan on January 15th. By January 23, 2020, China closed off Wuhan, and by the 31st the World Health Organization issued a Global Health Emergency. By February 3, 2020, the United States declared a public health emergency, and by March 11, the World Health Organization declared COVID-19 a pandemic. On March 13, 2020, President Trump declared a national emergency in the United States to begin releasing federal funding to fight the virus. On the same day, travel bans went into effect on non-U.S. citizens traveling from Europe.

Kentucky had its first confirmed case of COVID-19 on March 6, 2020 and a state of emergency was declared for the state. On March 11, 2020, Kentucky Governor Andy Beshear recommended that churches cancel services. A church (Star of Bethlehem Church) in Dawson Spring, just east of Paducah, held a revival with a visiting preacher from Texas on March 15 and 16, 2020 and the Hopkins County Health Department later linked at least 28 cases of COVID-19 and 2 deaths to this event, one of the first "super spreader" events in Kentucky.[2] By March 19, 2020, the Governor of Kentucky released an executive order against mass gatherings, which closed churches as well as schools and most other types of businesses. While many churches in Kentucky followed the governor's directives, there were a few which objected and refused to close in-person worship. Despite the governor's best efforts to invoke scripture itself, consistently arguing that this was a case of "loving our neighbors," a few vocal church leaders continued to resist.[3]

On April 12, 2020, the Maryville Baptist Church held an in-person Easter service in violation of Governor Beshear's orders and attendees were given a notice by the Kentucky State Police to self-quarantine for 14 days. The church went to court where the enforcement of the governor's order was halted until the governor amended the order on May 9, 2020 to allow services not exceeding 33% of the capacity of the building. June 10, 2020, this was raised to 50%. The Sixth Circuit Court ultimately rejected the attempt by the church to invalidate the executive orders on the grounds that they were no longer necessary, since the governor had already announced plans to reopen churches to limited in-person worship services on May 20, 2020. These plans were announced May 8, 2020 when there were 6,288 coronavirus cases and a total death count of 298 for the state of Kentucky.

The conflict with vocal church leaders was not over, however. Clays Mill Baptist Church in Jessamine County (the same county where Asbury Theological Seminary is located), led by Pastor Jeff Fugate,

---

[2] Bailey Loosemoore and Mandy McLaren, April 1, 2020, *Louisville Courier Journal*, "Kentucky county 'hit really, really hard' by church revival that spread deadly COVID-19" https://www.courier-journal.com/story/news/2020/04/01/coronavirus-kentucky-church-revival-leads-28-cases-2-deaths/5108111002/ Retrieved Jan. 5, 2021

[3] Lev. 19:18, quoted also by Jesus in Matt. 22:36-40 as one of the most important commandments.

defied Governor Andy Beshear's restrictions on in-person worship, which led to 18 members contracting the virus.[4] While most churches tried to find some way to continue ministry within this complex political environment, most of the attention went to the more vocal minority, and so the innovative attempts by many creative church leaders often went unnoticed or unrecognized. The point of this assignment was to bring those ideas and situations more to the surface and explore the theology that sustained these congregations.

On November 19, 2020, Governor Beshear requested churches to close for in-person services the following four Sundays through December 13, in order to mitigate the expected rise in cases from the Thanksgiving holidays. At this time the daily cases in Kentucky were 3,649 with 30 new deaths, the second highest day at that time in Kentucky. The governor did not attempt to mandate the actions of churches during this period of time, but the virus continued to surge throughout the state and the nation.

Theological Questions

In essence, I was intrigued by the potential theological questions raised by the pandemic, and so the assignment was designed to try and get to an understanding of how United States Christians in the middle of a pandemic were theologizing about the crisis. One can imagine a whole range of possible theological explanations, from Divine judgement to the work of Satan, and from a natural event to the End Times, and all the variations within these ranges. My mother's church in rural Maine (an independent Pentecostal church) fought against restrictions- holding services even when not recommended and ignoring social distancing with only minimal protections in place. Their view was that of the pandemic being a test of faith, one which they were determined to overcome by faith in God instead of the dictates of human authority. I knew from the Kentucky context, that this was a relative minority viewpoint among churches, so I was interested to find out what other churches were doing.

---

[4] Billy Kobin, June 9, 2020, *Louisville Courier Journal*, "Kentucky pastor spars with Beshear after 18 church members test positive for COVID-19" https://www.courier-journal.com/story/news/local/2020/06/09/coronavirus-kentucky-17-clays-mill-baptist-church-members-infected/3164299001/ Retrieved Jan. 5, 2021

During the time when most churches were closed, which fell during Easter- the high point of the Christian year for liturgical church communities, I must have watched four or five different worship services each week online. I watched everything from Greek Orthodox liturgies and Roman Catholic masses to Methodist, Baptist, Anglican, and Pentecostal services. I tried to include larger urban churches with an established online presence, as well as small rural congregations using their phones and Youtube to enter the age of digital ministry for the first time. I was fascinated by how each congregation tried to remain true to its tradition, but also sought to find new ways to create community and include innovative forms of ministry, like drive-through communion, drive-by parades of members (including one account of a drive-by Palm Sunday service where palms were passed out the day before so people could wave them), or drive-in services held outside while people stayed in their cars.

I am also connected, through my wife, to communities in El Salvador, and so I also kept my eye on the situation there. I was especially impressed by the traditional fiesta held in her hometown of Santa Ana in July. The Roman Catholic Church in El Salvador made good use of the devotion of the people to the images of saints, and so the saints were driven through the streets in place of the usual processions. The faithful stood at their doors and paid their devotion from a distance, sometimes in tears, as the priest and the saints passed by extending God's blessings to a people who were unable to gather or celebrate together.

All the while I kept trying to understand the situation theologically. My questions came down to five specific concerns:

1. **Lay and Pastoral Theology**. How are lay people and pastors trying to wrestle with the nature of God in the middle of this crisis? Are people exploring multiple churches online or focusing on the church they have traditionally identified with? How did this experience impact them personally in terms of their relationship with the Church, and did it impact their views on God?

2. **Pastoral Ministry**. How are pastors helping their congregations understand their situation theologically?

What are they communicating through videos, sermons, and songs? What are some of the difficulties they are facing?

3. **Innovative Ministry**. How are churches working to creatively continue maintaining contacts with their congregants while doors are closed and social distancing is encouraged? What does this ministry look like?

4. **Potential Impacts**. What are the concerns or thoughts about the future? Will things just go back to normal or will some lasting changes emerge from this crisis for the Church in the long term? How might the Church be impacted long-term?

5. **The *Missio-Dei* in the Pandemic**. One of the foundational ideas of Christian mission at this time is the theology of the *Missio-Dei*, that since the Father sent the Son, and the Father and Son sent the Spirit, so the Church has also been sent into the world to draw others back to God. How has this theology of sending been altered or changed by the current situation? How does the Church now see and understand its mission in the middle of a pandemic?

I worked to shape an assignment, which could explore these issues and still be utilized by students who were new to ethnographic methods. To get relatively similar case studies from each student, which could allow for some level of comparison, I developed the assignment with a high level of detail, including the questions to be asked. Here is the assignment, exactly as it was given to the students in both classes:

Online Congregational Study:
The Church's Response to Covid-19

Due to the corona virus crisis, for the summer of 2020 we will be doing a different ethnographic and congregational study than usual. So that we minimize the risk to everyone, we will be doing the project online. These special instructions will override all of the older instructions, which you might see in the course online (I don't want to remove all of these instructions since after this pandemic we will go back to the traditional assignment.) Essentially, we will be examining the Church's response to the Covid-19 epidemic.

Step One: You will need to choose a congregation which has an online presence. This must also be a church where you can contact the pastor online to answer some questions and get the response of at least two congregation members as well. Gather the following demographic information:

a. Denominational affiliation, if any.
b. Number of members.
c. Note if the location is rural, suburban, or urban.
d. Geographical area (and do some research about the Corona-virus outbreak in this area- was this area heavily impacted or not?).
e. Type of worship typically done (traditional, charismatic, contemporary, etc.)

Step Two: Watch the sermons of services for April 12, 19, 26, and May 3. Take notes to answer the following questions:

1. What was the scripture text used?
2. What music was used?
3. What as the main theme of the sermon?
4. Did the pastor tie the text to the Corona-virus pandemic? If so, how?
5. What seems to be the pastor's theological view of the pandemic?
6. How does the pastor feel the congregation should respond to the pandemic?
7. How might the choice of music relate to this theological position?
8. Take particularly good notes about when and how often the pastor connects his or her message to the pandemic.
9. Note anything else that might come to your attention as potentially significant.

Step Three: Contact the pastor online or by phone and have them answer the following questions, taking good notes of their responses:

10. When did your church stop having physical services, and when have they, (or will they) resume?
11. How did you make the decision to move to an online format?
12. Did you have a previous social media presence, and will you continue to have one after the pandemic?
13. What kinds of changes have you noticed in your congregation, especially while the services were online?
14. How did you attempt to minister to your congregation during the pandemic? Did you have any special services, outreach, or ministry opportunities?
15. Did you have to deal with any special circumstances, such as online weddings or figure out funeral arrangements in the middle of the pandemic?
16. Theologically, how do you think about the pandemic and its relations to God's work in the world?
17. Do you notice any changes in your congregation as a result of the pandemic when they returned to physical services? What are they?
18. Do you have any thoughts about the long-term effects of how the pandemic might change the way church is done in the future?
19. How do you think the pandemic has changed the way you personally see ministry and the way you meet your congregation's needs?

Step Four: Contact two congregation members online or by phone, with the permission of the pastor and ask the following questions, taking good notes of their responses:

20. Did you watch your church's online services each week during the pandemic? Why or why not?
21. Did you take the time to watch other church's services during the pandemic? Why or why not?
22. How did the absence of the physical church services affect you at this time?
23. How did you make the decision to return to the physical church service? Did you return as soon as the church opened or did you delay out of caution?
24. What, if any, role did God have in the pandemic?

25. How do you think the pandemic will affect your church in the future?
26. Has the pandemic changed your view of God any? How?
27. How well do you think your pastor adapted to the changes of moving the service online?
28. How did the pastor and/or the church reach out to you while there were no physical services?

Step Five: Turn in your answers to these questions and the demographic information when it is time to submit the ethnographic notes. It does not need to be written as a paper, just the answers. Be sure to make everything anonymous: make up a false name for the church, but one that might represent its denominational status. Do not give me a specific location, just tells me, "A church in rural Ohio, that has a traditional, United Methodist congregation of around 150 members," or something to that effect. In the same way, give the pastor a false name and the congregational members as well, but try to describe them accurately, "Pastor Jenny is an Episcopalian priest who has been the pastor of this congregation for five years, and was ordained 20 years ago. This is her third parish."

Step Six: Organize your information that you have gathered and write up your final paper to include the following sections:

a. Description of the church and congregation
b. Social Media ministry during the pandemic (including an analysis of the sermons for the four weeks)
c. Pastor's approach to ministry and theology of the pandemic
d. Effects on the congregation
e. Pandemic's potential impact on the future of this congregation
f. Personal reflections on this case and the *Missio Dei* of the Church

I am hoping if this assignment works well, we can publish them in a small book in First Fruits Press, which I oversee at the Seminary, so be sure they are as well written as possible. Don't wait to the last minute. Do not go over 20 pages or under 15 pages. Use 1-inch margins and 12-point Times New Roman font with footnotes for your citations instead of a works cited page. Be sure to cite any outside resources you use. If you have any questions, feel free to ask me as early as possible!

Concluding Thoughts

We set off on a journey of discovery together as a class. Along with the students and myself, we were also joined by my teaching intern, Greg S. Whyte (a Ph.D. student) for the Summer course. Greg, as a native of Canada, had returned to his home with his family, but he was an instrumental part of the journey online. He joins me in editing this volume, and I will let him bring everything together in the conclusion, as well as adding his own thoughts and experiences from across our northern border.

Do keep in mind as you read these chapters, they are not the work of seasoned anthropologists. In fact, most were doing ethnographic work for the very first time. Despite the challenges we faced, I am exceedingly proud of each and every one of them for the work they did. They surpassed my expectations in many ways and helped make this project something worthy of completing. Also keep in mind, those of you who may read this book in the future, that none of us knows the outcome of the COVID-19 crisis. We are writing in the middle of the crisis and do not have a crystal ball to show us what will emerge on the other side. We are simply capturing a snapshot of the Church in a critical moment of time. It could all dramatically shift tomorrow, but the one thing we all firmly believe is that God does not change and that God is the one who is in charge of all things, now and a hundred years from now, just as God was in charge in 1919 and in every epidemic in human history.

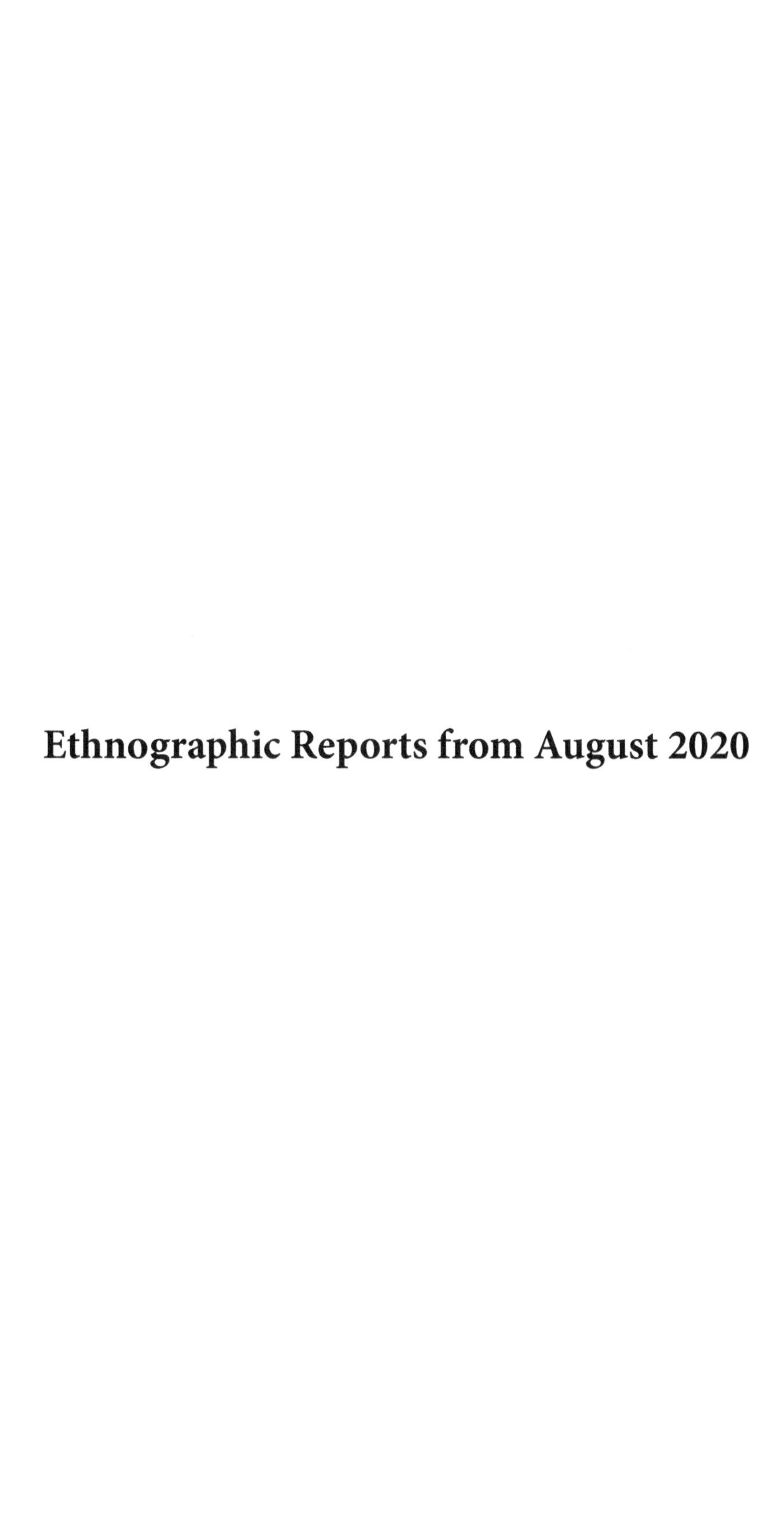

Ethnographic Reports from August 2020

Case Study One:
New Wine in New Wineskins

Rich Wardwell

Rich Wardwell serves as a Licensed Local Pastor in a United Methodist Church in South Georgia. After a nearly 30-year career in the technology industry, Rich is following God's calling into ministry while pursuing his M.Div. at Asbury Theological Seminary.

Context: Rural South Georgia
Affiliation: United Methodist
Size: 327 members (90 average attendance)

Introduction

The impact of COVID-19 on the church in the United States has been significant, if uneven. As communities began to see infections and the first deaths in March of 2020, governments and communities responded with varying degrees of lockdown and restrictions on movement and the social gathering of people. Christian churches in these communities came under both the legal impact due to COVID as well as moral responses to the pandemic. These decisions were complex, difficult, and dynamic, as the sparse data, changing government restrictions, and the shifting winds of community consensus created nearly impossible decisions.

For one church in a small rural community in South Georgia, the impacts of COVID and the response attempting to maintain some continuity of worship was no different. Complicated by a lack of technology and an older, potentially more virus-susceptible congregation, this church, like many, has been forced to make difficult decisions to pursue the continuity of the church in the best manner possible. Over the next few pages discussing this church, I will: describe the context of this church, review its immediate response to the pandemic, including examining four online sermons preached during April and early May of 2020, consider, based on interviews, both the pastor's approach during the pandemic and the impact on the congregation, and considerations for this church in the future. I will conclude with personal reflections on this church's response in light of the *Missio Dei* of the congregation.

Church Context

For a rural town in South Georgia centered in the heart of a farming region, world news, or even national news, often has a way of holding less relevance among the slow pace and local considerations of commodity crop prices and small-town politics. The community of approximately fifty-three hundred people also serves as the county seat, although considering the entire county only expands the population to just over seventeen thousand.[1] With the nearest metropolitan centers nearly three hours away (Atlanta to the north or Jacksonville to the south), it is easy to become detached from the goings on of the greater world. While a larger regional city, with a sizable university and a population of nearly one-hundred thousand, is only twenty-five miles away, this community and its inhabitants are fiercely self-sufficient and have fought hard to maintain their own hospital and shopping centers, Super Walmart, and a handful of fast-food and dine-in restaurants. The political leanings of the county are overwhelmingly conservative and match the self-sufficiency that permeates the community. Many have lived in this community for multiple generations — and these same generations have also deeply vested interests in their community's churches.

The church in this case sits just a block from the downtown core, serving as one of the town's larger churches, and one of a number of United Methodist Churches in the area. The church was organized in 1888, with its present building beginning construction in 1916.[2] Interestingly, the building was not completed until 1925, due to the flu epidemic of 1918. Currently, the church has three hundred and twenty-seven members, and, prior to the COVID pandemic, maintained an average attendance of nearly ninety attendees each Sunday. Sunday

[1] United Status Census Bureau, "Census Search."

[2] South Georgia Conference of the United Methodist Church, "Church Directory."

services are traditional in nature and are usually preceded by Sunday School meetings. The church body leans older in composition, although it was noted by congregants that after the recent retirement of a beloved established pastor, a younger preacher with a family of children was sought to attempt to engage a more diverse age group.

As a rural community, the town and county were initially not notably impacted by COVID and there were no positive cases for over a month while denser, populated areas, such as the neighboring county with its regional city were reporting infections. Significant infections would not become sustained in the church's county until June, months later. Even as of July 16, 2020, this county had only 271 confirmed cases (1554 cases per 100K), 4 total deaths and 28 hospitalizations.[3] In comparison, the neighboring county with a regional city had 2064 cases (1751 cases per 100K), 18 total deaths, and 108 hospitalizations. Even so, a unique event in the region impacted the early response and struck fear throughout the region. One of the very first super-spreader events in the United States occurred in Albany, Georgia, less than sixty miles away. Within weeks of two funerals, 490 were infected and 29 were dead, leading to one of the worst focused outbreaks in the entire country.[4] With little information or experience with COVID at that stage, surrounding communities were shaken. As the governor closed schools statewide, churches in the entire region quickly followed suit and closed almost simultaneously in the middle of March.

The church in this rural community shutdown in-person services in sync with nearly all the regional churches, concluding their last in-person service on March 15th. This also coincided with the Bishop of the United Methodist Church in South Georgia urging that all UMC churches in the South Georgia Annual Conference suspend in-person services as of March 16th.

In the following analysis, online services were observed on April 12th, 19th, 26th, and May 3rd. These four services began 4 weeks after the last in-person service. Each service was observed to analyze the logistical and spiritual responses made to maintain a continuity of

---

[3] Georgia Department of Public Health, "COVID-19 Daily Status Report."

[4] Chavez, Barajas, and Gallagher, "How Two Funerals Helped Turn One Small Georgia City into a Hotspot for Coronavirus."

mission within the church. In addition, the pastor of the church was interviewed, as well as two congregational members on a number of pre-determined questions considering the impacts and considerations of the pandemic and the church's response. In-person services returned for the church in this case study on June 21st.

Church Response & Social Media

Logistically, the church presented online streaming video and audio services solely via the Facebook platform. While these services were presented as livestreams within Facebook and released at the appropriate time Sunday morning, the AV materials were pre-recorded and edited in advance. As confirmed by the pastor during an interview, the church did not have pre-existing AV equipment to support livestream, or even for recording of video and audio. As COVID began to spread, equipment properly suited for churches to support even modest streaming became impossible to find — and still maintains limited availability even into late Summer. While the church maintained a social media presence on Facebook, livestream or deferred online services were not part of their preexisting capabilities.

To provide an online worship service, the pastor utilized the only equipment available to him. He used his iPhone, a tripod, and the church's Facebook account to present an online service. During the week, he would pre-record himself leading worship songs via guitar or piano, his sermon, and other elements, and then would edit them together for delivery on Sunday morning. The pastor varied how he utilized Facebook as he learned the ins and out of the social media platform, including *Premieres* that allow you to schedule and debut "live" a pre-recorded video, which is then saved to your church's Facebook page for later viewing. These services, from singing to the sermons, were recorded at a makeshift presentation area in front of the pulpit and altar to remain close to the fixed position iPhone and tripod.

The first service observed was on April 12th — Easter. This sermon, unlike the other three online services observed utilized pre-recorded segments of music and special interactions with various members of the laity edited into the service. This included a young child singing a song by Cher, *Love Can Build a Bridge*, a young man playing

Leonard Cohen's, *Hallelujah* on the trumpet, and a child reading 2 Timothy 1:7. The pastor spoke occasionally to the impacts of the current circumstances, including the cancellation of the Easter Egg Hunt in the announcements. During the traditional moment for the passing of the peace — the traditional face-to-face greeting — he presented a video of photos from different members of the congregation so the church could minimally see images of one another on Easter Sunday. This photo montage included contemporary Christian music in the background (*Known* by Tauren Wells) with what appeared to be a large portion of the congregation (at least 200+ people represented). Three other Christian songs were led by the pastor via guitar, singing Chris Tomlin's *Holy is the Lord*, Hillsong's *Worthy is the Lamb*, and the Gaither's, *Because He Lives.*

The primary theme of the sermon considered changing our perspective on the things of the world to the things above — the resurrected Jesus — and keeping our eyes on him through suffering and the tough times we may experience. The pandemic was rarely spoken to directly, but seemed implied by references to our current times that are "tough to lean into." The pastoral prayer spoke to the steadfastness of God and prayed for the health workers and all those that are helping the community make it through this difficult time. The pastor also noted at one point: "the building may be closed, but the church is alive and well..." While the Easter service clearly acknowledged the existing situation, it did not consider it in a significant theological manner. The pandemic appeared more like a short-term catastrophic event without long-term consequences or spiritual impacts that needed to be addressed.

The service of April 19th opened with the pastor speaking of opportunities for engagement within the church during this time, with various references to the existing circumstances: "Despite everything going on in our nation and world... that you have found some measure of peace and comfort... as we transition our service online... during this period of lock-down." These opportunities for engagement included a Pastor-led Tuesday devotional, *Thoughts & Thanks*, craft packets for kids, and a Zoom meeting for youth. He concluded these comments with a recurring statement from the previous service: "despite everything that is going on, the church is alive and well!"

The service music opened with the pastor leading, with an acoustic guitar, a rendition of Matt Redman's *Blessed Be Your Name.* After the Pastoral prayer, the pastor played a medley — which he noted as being intended for Easter, but weren't able to use then. This video was the pastor playing piano and singing a medley: *Because He Lives* by Gloria and Bill Gaither and *Arise My Love* by NewSong. The closing song was led by the pastor acapella, Andrae Crouch's *My Tribute* (*To God Be the Glory*). In the preparation for prayer, the pastor noted how much he missed seeing the congregation, and how we may have taken for granted the privilege and joy to worship together. The clear implication is that we should consider the value of church fellowship, community and worship together. The pastoral prayer spoke again to the current unprecedented period that we are within (without specifically naming it), thanked and prayed blessings on the healthcare and government officials struggling with hard decisions, and the time where we could return again to being able to worship together.

The sermon focused primarily on the story of Thomas and his need to see Jesus's scars before he would believe. During the reading of the passage in John 20:19-20, the pastor referred to the situation of the disciples after the crucifixion — discouraged, gathered in isolation and fear behind closed doors. He then asked the viewers if they can relate to this, based on "what is going on within our world" and spoke to the hope available as Jesus seeks the disciples out, which should give the viewers encouragement as we continue in isolation. Outside this moment early in the sermon, there were no mention of the pandemic or application of the message to the current events outside a reminder of Jesus's humanity and suffering. Notably, through the announcements and the sermon, the pastor never spoke the words Coronavirus, COVID or pandemic outside somewhat vague references to its effects.

The third service observed on April 26th introduced the first extensive engagement with the pandemic. In the pastoral prayer, he continued to pray for essential personnel — something repeated in each service — but a notable change included the reference, "in this time of pandemic." This appears to be the first time that the specific cause for the struggles and troubling times has been noted. He also mentioned a praise that a member tested negative for COVID-19 — the first time that the pandemic's causal virus had been named — and not the last time in this service. The initial opening song was led by the pastor with an acoustic guitar — *What A Savior* by Laura Story. The concluding hymn was Be *Thou My Vision.*

The sermon focused on the story of Jesus on the Emmaus Road after His resurrection, speaking to our inability to always recognize God, noting that we can be in Jesus's presence and not even recognize it. We are urged to get rid of our idols and obstacles so that we can refocus on God and His heart. The last third of the sermon moved from the Emmaus Road to a complete engagement of the pandemic. First, the events of the pandemic are addressed as a way of "zapping" our passion for God, but then denotes that our issues of lack of passion started long before COVID-19 — and can't be blamed on it. The sermon then pivots to the positive benefits of the current COVID world —slower pace, families spending time together, cleaner air, etc. The pastor then directs the listener that we should not desire the old normal and challenges us to consider the lessons God has taught us in this time of pandemic, such as God's presence as priority over our activities and the things of this world. We should never go back to some of the things that we left behind. As the world has become jaded and negative, we must also not fall into that pattern but approach God like a child. We must remove the idols and approach God in a fresh way.

This is the first sermon that considered the pandemic as a primary character within it. The pandemic was utilized as both an element of negative impact, as well as an element of change - that we could use this time to reset — a refocus and renewal — a new passion for Jesus Christ. Additionally, the pastor spoke specifically and very briefly to a future reopening of the church. He quoted Wesley's, "do no harm, do good, and stay in love with God" — and that when reopening does occur, they would focus on doing no harm. He noted that in the upcoming weeks, meetings would be scheduled with leadership to discuss what would be necessary to reopen in the future.

The final service of May 3rd continued the focus on the pandemic begun on April 26th. The pastor introduced this sermon as one that he expected to give as soon as COVID-19 began due to its focus on perseverance and endurance. Even the music was prefaced with its implications to our time of pandemic. The opening song was led by the pastor with an acoustic guitar — *Yes I Will* by Vertical Worship — a popular contemporary worship song that reminds us that God will never fail us and that we should choose to praise Him in all circumstances. When introducing the song, the pastor specifically noted that it was applicable to our current times because no matter what our circumstances are and our lack of control over them, we do have control over our ability to praise and trust God. The hymn, *Leaning on the Everlasting Arms* was sung after the pastoral prayer. *It is Well With My Soul* was sung at the end of the sermon. Finally, the service closed with Blessed Assurance, a hymn of great comfort.

The sermon read from James 1:2-8 and focused on our need to count it joy when we experience trials and suffering. The joy is not in the suffering itself — but in what is to be gained, learned or revealed in it. It also produces endurance that cannot be gained any other way — a time of growth as God works in and through the trials. God is present with us. Throughout the sermon, the pastor paralleled the suffering and trials in the passage in James to our own situation in the pandemic and our responses to it. We all are experiencing some aspects of emotional, physical and mental impacts — suffering and trial — during the times of this pandemic. God is present with us in suffering — and we are to be examples to the world in a time such as this. While the pastor speaks to feelings of uselessness due to our inability to "go and do" for the Kingdom, we are reassured that staying at home and wearing a mask is the loving, compassionate thing to do: "It's ok to be ok right now."

Throughout the four weeks, a very clear progression is noted as the services each week grow in reference and consideration of the pandemic, both in the lives of the individuals of the church, the church's response, and God's role within. While the first two services did not even name the events that were impacting the church, the third began to address the pandemic and the fourth provided direct guidance and response for the Christian during this specific period of lockdown and pandemic.

Pastoral Approach

After watching the four online sermons, as I met with the Pastor to ask a number of questions on his response to the pandemic, I felt a bit like I was speaking to a superhero. Over the previous months, this pastor had not only preached sermons, but built a streaming technology platform out of the proverbial bailing wire, acted as producer, video camera operator, sound technician, worship director, guitarist, pianist, and singer. The passion for his church, his congregation, and for the continuity of God's mission within was palpable. For this pastor, the decision to move online wasn't a question — the people needed to have a means to hear the word — "the church needs to continue."

The passion of the pastor seemed to be rewarded, as the pastor praised the faithfulness of the people in attending and giving during the period of online worship. He even noted that many of his elderly, who were not technical, were willing to create Facebook accounts, purely to be engaged with the church. In addition to the service, the pastor also began an online devotional, "Tuesday's Thoughts and Thanks" that goes online at 11:30am each Tuesday and which has continued even after the reopening of in-person church services. He also noted that the church has persisted with outreach and ministry in the community, including giving out food, helping those in need, and engaging the community.

As far as a theological response for the actions of the church in this time, the pastor cited Mark 2 and the analogy of new wine and new wineskins — the church needs to be a new wineskin. The church is being forced to recognize the value of an online presence, but also is stirring a hunger for community in-person. His hope is that current circumstances will force the church to rediscover its lost traditional elements — embodied, lived out, engaged in community.

As in-person services have returned, attendance has been only 1/3rd of its pre-COVID numbers. Fortunately, the pastor noted that the streaming service is still seeing a significant response. Somewhat paradoxically, the pastor observed that the retired and elderly are those who have been most likely to return to in-person services. Those who are the most vulnerable to the pandemic's effects seem to be the group most faithful to being at church. This poses a number of questions and potential conclusions. The pastor believes this is primarily related to the younger people being more comfortable with technology. Even with reduced attendance, giving to the church has remained "good", but not at pre-COVID levels.

Some of the most moving comments from the pastor related to the experience of ministry and the ineffectiveness in meeting congregational needs. He noted it has been difficult to experience church that's not embodied and outward focused: "there is no substitute for in-person worship." The importance of engaging community has been highlighted in the time of separation — and the lack of communion was mentioned specifically.

Congregational Response

Two congregation members in the observed church were interviewed to analyze the effects of the COVID response by the church. While both members participated actively in the online services presented during the suspension of in-person services, only one has chosen to return to in-person services now that they are available. Both expressed the necessity to experience church during the lockdown period, and online was the only option available. Neither appeared to have much desire to watch sermons from churches other than their home church, although one noted they watched others occasionally, "out of curiosity." Both expressed appreciation for the convenience offered — to livestream at the traditional service time or to defer watching until another time — although both appeared to watch the service on Sunday.

As noted, when in-person services finally returned, the two congregants differed substantially in response. One congregant had been involved in the committee on reopening the church and had a high confidence of safety, which seemed to be of ultimate concern. The other, while not concerned about safety, expressed a lack of interest in returning to church in the current environment.

Both congregants praised the response of the pastor and the church. Each believed the pastor had been handed a very difficult situation and had responded innovatively in providing continuity through online services. One noted that they doubted the previous pastor would have had the expertise or resources to innovate an online solution in the difficult technical environment.

Neither congregant felt that COVID had changed their view of God. God is still sovereign. One even noted that God had used the pandemic for His good, allowing people to engage with their families and find time to rest and learn to reconnect with family and a simpler life (a theme within one of the online services). The other noted only one suggestion for improvement — the engagement of more laity in the online services to make it feel more like "normal church." As noted in the analysis of services, the Easter services did engage significant laity, but was otherwise absent from all the other services analyzed.

As a small community church, communication via member-to-member contact has continued throughout the pandemic, but the observed church seems to have relied heavily on Facebook to communicate with members. This includes regular postings and updates from the pastor, a weekly livestreamed homily, and the Sunday service.

As noted, as in-person services have resumed, one congregant had returned, and one had not. This again did not appear to be due to safety concerns, but, rather, due to the convenience factor of online services. The congregant who has not returned noted that he was more of an introvert and the things that most people grieve as lost in an online service don't have a lot of value for him. He noted that he doesn't enjoy the social aspects or the singing. While prior attendance during in-person times was not an inquiry, the perception was that this congregant may actually hear more sermons overall due to online now being an option.

Post-Pandemic Future

As the pandemic has proceeded, the church in this case has returned to a diminished in-person service with restrictions and no Sunday School, choir, or nursery. A quick anecdotal survey of churches in the area provided a wide array of responses. Some divisions in response appeared to be denominational in nature, as Baptist churches seemed to generally open sooner and with less restriction, while Methodist churches opened later. Others appeared to be related to the general age demographic of the congregation, with younger congregations tending to open earlier and more fully. Race also seems to provide some delineation, as most African American churches generally are still closed to in-person services. Of course, church openings and restrictions seem to vary greatly geographically as well.

Entering the late summer of 2020, while schools are opening in-person, churches in the area are occasionally closed due to outbreaks, including one church blocks away from the studied church that impacted a large portion of the body and resulted in a related death. Yet, most churches continue to operate in-person services, but rarely more than that. Nurseries, Sunday Schools and other church activities are still generally curtailed, although a number of churches are beginning to venture into these areas, including the hosting of a large youth weekend at a UMC church in the neighboring county (a younger skewed, contemporary-styled church).

When interviewing the pastor of the observed church, in-person services had returned in the preceding weeks on June 21st. While taking a conservative approach similar to the United Methodist Church as a whole, he noted a clear anticipation that church would likely not return to any semblance of normal in 2020 and maybe even into 2021. Nursery, in-person Sunday School, choir, and many other aspects of the in-person Sunday worship service and weekly ministries is still on hold. The pastor spoke of potential ministry opportunities in the future — including online Bible study groups and meetings, but was not planning any further extensions to in-person activities at this time. The clear focus on the near-term future is to expand and develop the online presence, including consideration of dedicated hardware and equipment to improve the livestream capability of the church, which is still utilizing the original system of iPhone, tripod, and Facebook. The pastor believed that online worship was no longer an option, but a critical component of all churches that needed to be embraced. He also noted that this opens up questions on measuring engagement — that the online formulas have altered the church's numbers in a very positive way, but this doesn't seem to effectively measure the local context. One final question noted by the pastor seemed very prescient — what is to be gained by the people being in church? This question is one that certainly needs an answer in the future church.

The congregants interviewed provide an interesting perspective on the future of the church. One congregant enjoyed online services but eagerly looked forward to the opportunity to worship in-person, and quickly engaged in in-person services when they began in June. The second congregant also enjoyed online services — to the extent that they expressed little desire to return to in-person services (and had not done so at the time of interview). Both believed that the immediate impacts of the pandemic and shutdown of in-person services to the church would be negative. The one congregant who looked forward to the return to in-person services was concerned about restrictions on touching, hugging, and social distancing that would reduce the fellowship and experience as well as fears of safety in the close quarters of a church building. Both expressed concern that many would never return to church in-person again, although one was more concerned about safety and the medically fragile, while the other believed that many would prefer the convenience and ease of church from home and time-savings offered.

Reflection & the *Missio Dei*

The struggles facing church leaders today is an immensely difficult one. For pastors and church leaders, the strain caused by the heavy burden of the juxtaposition of the critical nature of the mission of the church on one side and the safety and love of people (particularly those most fragile) on the other, is immense. The political climate that envelops these decisions also means that any response will likely result in significant negative reactions from a portion of the church body and community. There are no "good" answers and any answer will be heavily resisted, sometimes quite violently. Depending on seemingly uncontrollable events, even when abiding by the severest of restrictions, opening or engaging in different aspects of in-person ministry may result in infection that may risk death for loved ones. Not opening may negatively impact souls and suspend the activity of the church and the activity of the mission of the church as instruments of God to reconcile the world to Him. A common refrain from pastors and leaders of other organizations: until you have been placed in the unenviable position to make these types of decisions, you do not feel the full burden and weight of the consequences in either direction.

To add further concern to the current situation, based on the congregants interviewed here and continued observations in other contexts, a mounting deep concern is becoming apparent — that a meaningful portion of the body of Christ no longer values in-person worship. The longer that the body is separated, the more this division may increase. This may be revealing the invasiveness of moralistic therapeutic deism within the modern Western church — a pluralistic belief system that believes that people just "need to be good" and the central goal of life is to be happy. Combining this with an American affair with individualism leads to a deeply individualized, me-centered faith that thinks little of the communal aspects, love for neighbor, or the need for relationship and the Church as described in the Bible. This self-help faith leads to church hopping, church shopping, and now, very easily, an online church of convenience. Whether due to the moralistic therapeutic deism or just cultural shifts, the paradox in the observed church of the most vulnerable elderly being the primary group willing to return to in-person service is disturbing.

The church is certainly in a transformational age. Unfortunately, the next months are hard to decipher, as the pandemic continues, exacerbated by the significant divisiveness in America and tribalism, as a lost people search for identity. The church must find its foundational footing in the *Missio Dei* — God's mission for His people. A stagnant, feel good, inward looking church will likely find it difficult in the proceeding months and years to survive and flourish. Unless it is actively pursuing the reconciliation of creation to God through active and dynamic Holy Spirit filled ministry and a holistic embrace of both evangelism and service, the church will struggle as it strays from God's mission for His people. This pursuit may include both a revisiting of old lost tradition that needs to be recovered, the dismissal of more recent traditions that no longer relate well to our current cultural context, and the embracing of new traditions that fully engage an everchanging contemporary cultural context.

Works Cited

Chavez, Nicole, Angela Barajas, and Dianne Gallagher. "How Two Funerals Helped Turn One Small Georgia City into a Hotspot for Coronavirus." CNN, 2020. https://www.cnn.com/2020/04/02/us/albany-georgia-coronavirus/index.html.

Georgia Department of Public Health. "COVID-19 Daily Status Report," 2020. https://dph.georgia.gov/covid-19-daily-status-report.

South Georgia Conference of the United Methodist Church. "Church Directory," 2020. https://www.sgaumc.org.

United Status Census Bureau. "Census Search," 2020. https://www.census.gov.

Case Study Two:

Spiritual Communion in a Socially Distanced World

Alyssa Cowart Behrman

After graduating from Kennesaw State University in 2016 Alyssa returned to her home church in Middle Georgia to serve as a Student Director. After graduating from ATS in 2020, Alyssa, with her husband and high school sweetheart Andrew, will move to Europe where they will unite their loves of ministry and travel.

Context: Suburban Middle Georgia
Affiliation: Roman Catholic
Size: 550 families in the parish

Introduction

When the "coronavirus disease of 2019" (COVID-19) first appeared in the United States in early 2020, life radically changed for many individuals, families, and organizations. Businesses closed their doors, airports shut down, and families were urged to stay inside their homes unless making an "essential" trip, such as to a grocery store. The pandemic surrounding COVID-19 has forced some organizations to shut down permanently; others have had to temporarily halt activities; and yet others have had to innovate or pivot. Churches and other faith communities around the United States are facing the same choices and struggles.

Church Context

Georgia has been one of the worst states in the US when it comes to containing the spread of COVID-19. As of the moment I write this, the "Peach" state has had over 206,000 confirmed cases with over 4,200 deaths.[1] In the middle of the state sits a county known for its large military base and a good school system. This county, in the heart of Georgia, has a population of around 100,000, that is made up of primarily working-class families. The spread of COVID-19 has not been as severe in this area as in some larger, surrounding counties, claiming over 2,000 confirmed cases and over 60 deaths. Still, the hospitals are overwhelmed and the community is rattled .

It's not uncommon to find people in this county who have been born and raised in the Middle Georgia area. Others have been brought to the region by their armed forces affiliation, but have stayed to retire or raise their family. Situated within the "Bible-Belt," this Middle Georgia community is home to many churches, and most families claim the Christian faith. In a county like this one, when a church closes its doors, people take notice. Like most places in the United States, this Middle Georgia county has seen churches young and old close, stall, and pivot during the pandemic.

"Saint Patty" Catholic Church sits on a small piece of land right off a busy road in suburban Middle Georgia. The parish sits across the street from a country club with a pond and a family friendly neighborhood. Although situated in a nice and convenient part of town, the parish is not lavish. There is no flashy sign at the edge of the property, no large ornate steeple, not even a clear marker at the entrance. A quick turn off the main road and there you are, sitting in the small parking lot of "Saint Patty" Catholic Church. The landscaping is simple, but well maintained. A few small statues of saints align the narrow path that leads from the parking lot to the main entrance. In the summer and spring, flowers bloom outside the front doors. In this Middle Georgia community, there are very large and very small church structures that line the roads, often right next to or across from one another. By comparison, "Saint Patty"'s

---

1 "COVID-19 Status Report." *Georgia Department of Public Health*, dph.georgia.gov/covid-19-daily-status-report. Data retrieved August 10, 2020.

church building is medium sized. The exterior is plain, appearing more modest than other Catholic Churches in the area.

While the front doors of the church's structure are the first point of contact for some members and visitors, the church's website is the new place of first impressions. For many people, their first interactions with a faith community is digital. Convenience and low stakes have made a quick Google search the path of many to discovering a church home. Now, during a time of pandemic, where normal activities like attending a church service, have higher risks associated with them, online presence is even more important. Saint Patty's website, in many ways, mirrors the image of their campus. The website is functional but not beautiful, easy to navigate but not engaging. It is clearly maintained similarly to the lawn. Information is updated, but nothing flashy is added. The website is one of the first to appear when doing an online search for Catholic Churches in the area. Physically and digitally, the parish, modest and cared for, is easy to find.

Here, Father E. pastors his flock. "Saint Patty" is home to five-hundred and fifty families that are registered as members of the parish. Along-side Father E. serves Reverend Mr. J., a Deacon at "St. Patty." For the safety of their parish members Father E. and Deacon J. stopped holding in-person services, including weekends and weekday mass, funerals, weddings, baptisms, catechesis, and all other physical church activities on March 16, 2020. This closure of "St. Patty"'s building has had consequences, both positive and negative. The pressure of making that decision did not rest solely on Father E. or Deacon J., however. "Saint Patty" Catholic Church is a part of the Savannah Diocese, and so was directed to halt physical services and church programs by the Bishop of Savannah. When this guidance from the Bishop was given to Father E. and Deacon J., they had to decide how to continue caring for parishioners in a new way. Like millions of other churches, businesses, and organizations, "Saint Patty" had to pivot.

Church Response & Social Media

A tool in the hands of most church leaders in the United States of America is the internet. "Saint Patty," like many other churches, had a website and Facebook page before the start of the pandemic, though these digital resources did not get much attention from the church leaders or from parishioners. When the parish was able to meet together in person, Father E. managed the Facebook page. He would post infrequently, usually information to celebrate a saint on their given day. According to Father E., interaction with people, parish members and non-members, was rare and little energy was dedicated to change that - until a world-wide pandemic happened. What was once a low impact hobby of one priest became a golden life-line connecting "Saint Patty" Church with parishioners once the building had to close. So, Father E. and Deacon J. worked to learn the neglected technology and moved quickly to utilize it.

Starting out with a single iPhone, Deacon J. began to broadcast special events of the church. At first, these livestreams were short messages from Father E. to parishioners. Then Deacon J. began to record and post videos of funerals for parishioners and family members or friends of the deceased. Finally, celebrations of the Mass were livestreamed on Facebook. All of this recording and streaming took place entirely on an iPhone at the start. As one may assume, shooting lengthy events and services on an iPhone presents challenges. Although it was convenient, the iPhone videos had unreliable sound, sometimes going completely out for an extended period of time. Facing these issues, Father E. and Deacon J. discovered good news and bad news. The good news was that people were watching the videos. They were interacting together in the comments section, and they were expressing gratitude for feeling connected once again to their faith community. The bad news was that their simple iPhone recording was not meeting their new digital ministry needs.

Deacon J., who has worked with technology in the past, set to work to improve the online worship experience for his beloved parish. With a few additions to their technological lineup, which included audio equipment, a repurposed laptop, and a video camera, the quality of "Saint Patty"'s online experience quickly improved. With the adjustments made, recording and streaming services became more regular, and to Father E. and Deacon J.'s pleasure, more and more parishioners began to regularly join the online community. Not only were these church leaders able to see the faces of those families who would usually be sitting in their sanctuary digitally, but they were also seeing families and individuals that had long since moved away from the area. In this way, the pandemic has given "Saint Patty" Catholic Church a larger platform for ministry and has made their community international.

Although many parishioners are taking advantage of the online worship experience that "Saint Patty" is offering (estimated by Father E .to be about 300 families who participate regularly online), not all 550 families are represented online. If playing by the normal rules of in-person worship, this fact would be a major problem in the eyes of Father E. and Deacon J. The Catholic Church requires their members to attend mass weekly to remain free from sin, but due to the pandemic, the parish members have been given dispensation, a pardon from attending mass, until the end of August (although that could be extended). For this reason, Father E. and Deacon J. affirm that those members not participating in online mass are still able to remain free from sin but should join online as they are able for their own spiritual cultivation.

During the online worship services, there is a lot of music. "Saint Patty" is a musical church who enjoys a contemporary style. In most videos, a single woman with an acoustic guitar leads the hymns and songs of praise, which are dispersed throughout the service. Each service contains reading from scripture, a message or short sermon, and prayer. For some churches in the Middle Georgia area, this covers all the bases for what they expect from a church service. For Roman Catholics, however, some key elements are missing. Confession and Eucharist are vital parts of the spiritual life of this faith community. Since neither confession nor Eucharist can be done virtually through a Facebook livestream, "Saint Patty" has continued to adapt and innovate to meet the spiritual needs of the parish.

The Catholic Church celebrates seven sacraments: Eucharist, baptism, confirmation, matrimony (marriage), anointing of the sick, reconciliation (confession), and ordination. Each of these sacraments, or sacred events, represents the theology of "Saint Patty" Catholic Church. These sacraments represent important events in the life of a believer, and in a church as vibrant as "Saint Patty," these events represent a calendar year's worth of celebrations for the entire parish. In Georgia, the sacraments of the Catholic Church have been largely disrupted, due to social distancing guidelines from the CDC (Center for

Disease Control) in Atlanta and from Governor Kemp.[2] Six-feet is the recommended distance to keep from others, and group meetings, for a time, were limited to only ten people.[3] These regulations have meant that Eucharist cannot continue as normal, since the touching of elements and close proximity create a much higher risk of contamination. Weddings and ordinations have been performed with only ten people present (included in that number are the bride, groom, and priest) or have been livestreamed to take the celebration digital. Celebrations of baptism and confirmation have been postponed at "Saint Patty." Anointing of the sick (and final rites) is done on a case-by-case basis, sometimes being performed over the phone instead of in-person.

Congregational Response

Of these sacraments, the celebration of the Eucharist is perhaps the most missed by the parishioners of "Saint Patty." Amongst those church members, yearning to receive communion traditionally again is Parishioner L., a woman in her mid -sixties who has spent her working years in local Middle Georgia classrooms, and who has spent almost every weekend of the past twenty years in "Saint Patty" Catholic Church. Parishioner L. is a social woman. She loves greeting friends with a warm hug, participating in church events, and is deeply committed to her parish. Like other parishioners, Parishioner L. and her husband have spent their pandemic Sundays watching "Saint Patty" services via the link on the Church's website. Although she feels a sense of connection from the digital experience, especially to Father E. and Deacon J., who have been pastoring her for years, it is not the same. In addition to her participation in Sunday worship with "Saint Patty," Parishioner L. also tunes into the digital service streamed by the Catholic Church of her youth in Alabama. She loves seeing familiar faces from the parish she grew up in, the parish where her faith was first developed.

---

[2] "Governor Kemp Calls on Georgians to Do 'Four Things for Four Weeks' to Stop COVID-19." *Governor Brian P. Kemp Office of the Governor,* gov.georgia.gov/press-releases/2020-07-21/governor-kemp-calls-georgians-do-four-things-four-weeks-stop-covid-19. Retrieved August 10, 2020.

[3] "COVID-19: Unite to Stop the Spread." *Georgia.gov,* georgia.gov/covid-19-coronavirus-georgia/covid-19-state-services-georgia/covid-19-unite-stop-spread. Retrieved August 10, 2020.

While the COVID-19 pandemic has brought feelings of sadness, fear, and isolation for Parishioner L. and her husband, the couple does not feel that they have suffered spiritually. Parishioner L. shared with me that while she is starved socially, she feels as though the pandemic has brought her deeper into connection with God. Though missing her church building and the people that normally fill it, Parishioner L. says that she has been made more aware of God in her daily activities and has found herself praying more often and more naturally during the pandemic. "Because of the pandemic," Parishioner L. shares, "I am more aware of my need for God throughout every day." Her reflections have led Parishioner L. to believe that "God is holding us up during this pandemic." She notes that lock-down in the Middle Georgia area first occurred during the Lenten season, which for her is significant because "If God sent His son Jesus to suffer, I can endure this suffering."

While desperately missing the hugs, smiles, and activities that accompany the in-person "Saint Patty" Church experience, Parishioner L. cannot say enough good things about the way her leaders, Father E. and Deacon J., have handled the pandemic. She says that the church staff has been "tweaking" and improving the digital experience since the start. "They have moved quickly," says L., "the solid stuff I am accustomed to getting from sermons has not waivered." All updates and church information are sent out via email, which Parishioner L. says, gives you all the information you need to be an informed parishioner of "Saint Patty" during this time.

On May 25th "Saint Patty" Catholic Church re-opened their doors for socially-distanced in-person services. The reopening date was again given to Father E. from the Bishop of Savannah, the head of the Savannah Diocese, which "Saint Patty" is a part of. With this new information Parishioner L. and her husband, as well as all "Saint Patty" parishioners, had to make a decision whether or not they would return to the church building or remain online. Although a social butterfly, for Parishioner L. and her husband, in-person services were not a safe option. Parishioner L. suffers from MS (Multiple sclerosis) and her husband has an ongoing heart condition. She also shared that both she and her husband are overweight and that the risk is too high for them to return to the church building until the pandemic is better contained. Parishioner L. predicts that when it is safer to return that the church will be quite different, with less hugs and more health precautions in place. She prays that she will be able to return safely soon, to rejoin the physical faith community she loves, but most of all, to take communion, the thing she has missed the most during the pandemic.

Missing the Eucharist most of all, Parishioner K. and his wife are also long-term "Saint Patty" members who have loyal affection for their faith community. Another teacher in the county school system, Parishioner K. says the transition to online services has been natural and seamless. "As soon as an online option was available," remarks K., "we joined in." Although they were early adapters to the virtual church shift, Parishioner K. and his wife made the decision to return to in-person meetings at "Saint Patty" as soon as the church building re-opened on May 25th. With no major health concerns that would delay their immediate reentry to the physical parish and a new school year just around the corner (a year in which K. fully intends to teach his classes in-person), the couple said that moving back to regular meetings felt natural, since they had stayed connected virtually throughout the time away.

Like L., Parishioner K. expresses pride and gratitude in the way Father E. and Deacon J. have responded to the pandemic. K. notes that Deacon J. is good with technology and was able to make the transition to online happen quickly. The parish staff communicates frequently with parishioners via email and Facebook, making it possible to remain a fully engaged and active parishioner, even during this world health crisis. For K. and his wife, the online experience was "good, very good, but cannot replace truly being there, seeing the icons, and taking communion together." Celebrating the Eucharist was a driving factor for the couple's return in May, as it was for many who returned to the parish.

Church Response & the Sacraments

Returning to physical meetings was not a viable option for most in May, and remains too high a risk for many, like Parishioner L. and her husband. To meet the spiritual need and desire of the parish to participate in the Eucharist, Father E. and Deacon J. have introduced a new method of celebrating the sacrament that can be conducted virtually, "spiritual communion." Spiritual communion is offered over the Facebook livestream and website recording during every Mass where Eucharist would normally be celebrated. This "virtual sacrament" is offered through a prayer allowing parishioners to receive the blessing of communion at home without being present for the sacrament and without using any elements. All those not able to be present at the Mass can join the prayer, led by Deacon J., which expresses the intention to experience the sacrament while not accessing sacred elements. To invite viewers into this act of spiritual communion, Deacon J. prays these words: "My Jesus, I believe that You are present in the Most Holy Sacrament. I love you above all things, and I desire to receive You into my soul. Since I cannot at this moment receive You sacramentally, come at least spiritually into my heart. I embrace You as if You were already there and unite myself wholly to You. Never permit me to be separated from You. Amen."

Another sacrament whose method has been modified to accommodate new COVID-19 health guidelines is reconciliation, better known as the act of confession.[4] While Father E. expresses confidence in his parishioner's ability to live without mortal sin, at least for the time of the pandemic, he has thought it necessary to continue offering confession. Instead of the usual confessional set-up, the sacrament takes place in one of the parish's many classrooms which is normally used for Sunday School, but now has been transformed for safety and privacy. Sheets and room dividers separate a space in the classroom which allows Father E. to hear confessions without a great risk of spreading COVID-19 through droplets, spray, or touch. A small but powerful air purifier with UV light sits in the classroom, and any surfaces that Father E. or parishioners come into contact with is sanitized after confession has concluded. Before parishioners can enter the building to be escorted to the classroom for confession, they are stopped at the front entrance to do a few quick health checks. The church receptionist, V., invites guests and members into the building after making sure they are wearing a mask, taking their temperature to ensure they do not have a fever, and asking them to use the large container of hand sanitizer that the parish has provided.

[4] "Considerations for Communities of Faith." *Centers for Disease Control and Prevention*, Centers for Disease Control and Prevention, www.cdc.gov/coronavirus/2019-ncov/community/faith-based.html. Retrieved August 10, 2020.

While events such as weddings, ordination, and baptism have been postponed until they can be publicly celebrated safely, catechetical training has been able to continue via Zoom video conferencing. Final rites and anointing of sick parishioners has been done over the phone, although Father E. says that he would be willing to perform those duties in person at a parishioner's request. Besides the sacraments, "Saint Patty" has been able to continue ministering in other ways. The food ministry of "Saint Patty", for example, has been thriving during this time. Parishioners can continue to give financially through the website and special funds are even collected virtually for pandemic relief. Through this effort, "Saint Patty" Catholic Church has been able to do ministry by way of food ministry to people in the Middle Georgia community and around the globe.

The ministry that has had to adapt the least due to the COVID-19 virus is the preaching of the Word. Although the method of delivering sermons and services has changed for "Saint Patty," the content and structure of those services has not been altered. Some of the first recorded services that are posted to the "Saint Patty" Facebook page are from April 12th, May 6th, May 11th, and May 16th. These four recordings represent an Easter Celebration, a Mother's Day Vigil (5th Sunday of Easter Vigil), a weekday Mass, and a 6th Sunday of Easter Vigil. These streamed services are lively with many times for song and music. Each service was begun and concluded with a hymn and there is generally time for singing between scripture reading, the preaching, and other points of transition in the service. The songs are generally short and upbeat. Sections of "They Will Know Us By Our Love," "Hail, Holy Queen," "Glory to God in the Highest," and "This is the Day that the Lord has Made" can be expected. Contrary to the solemn atmosphere one might expect from a church in a pandemic, the services at "Saint Patty" are cheery. The choices of music reflect a sense of peace and desire to praise God for His goodness in any situation.

In addition to the music lead with hymn books and instruments is the singing that directs various other parts of the service. It is common at "Saint Patty" Catholic Church for the parish to join in singing The Lord's Prayer instead of reciting it. Deacon J. can also be counted on to pray and direct the service through song. Each note sung out is joyful and worshipful. Even when coming from a single voice over a video recording, viewers can imagine the united voices of the entire parish joining together in song to say "Lord, hear our prayer."

The energetic atmosphere of the videos is made even more positive by the comments that fill the right side of viewers screens. Throughout the service, comments from parishioners who viewed the message live scroll down with greetings, "amens," and comments on the sermon. While the comments section is not the same time of greeting that parishioners are used to, it serves as a vehicle for virtual fellowship during these live-steam videos.

As with the choice of hymns over these four weeks, the selection of scripture and the main themes of the sermon were not hyper focused on the pandemic. In fact, quite the contrary. Three of the four sermons on these dates do not explicitly mention COVID-19 or it's effect, except during prayer. As might be expected, the April 12th scripture text and message were focused on the Easter celebration, the resurrection of Jesus. It was not until about half-way through the service that the first mention of the pandemic came, when Deacon J. rose to the podium to pray. In this Easter service, as in the other three services here discussed, Deacon J. spends time mid-service leading the parish in prayer. In song, Deacon J. prays to God for safety during the pandemic, for all families of the parish, for protection over all first responders and essential workers. He prayerfully sings to ask for mercy for all victims of the pandemic, including those suffering with illness, those suffering financially, those suffering from loneliness, and those displaced. In some services Deacon J. prays for strength for leaders around the world and that they would use their resources for peace. The Deacon also prays for those already deceased. After each line of the Deacon's prayer, the few parishioners in the building that can be heard on the video recording sing "Lord, Hear Our Prayer."

While lifting up the most vulnerable in prayer, Deacon J. also adamantly prays for an end to the COVID-19 virus and the effect of the pandemic. This may have indicated that Deacon J., and the parish, believe that God is in control and still listening to the prayers of His people. The belief that God is powerful, good, and deserving of praise even during a world-wide pandemic is implicit in the sermons from April 12th, May 6th, and May 11th, but is made explicit on May 16th.

During the May 16th service, Deacon J. brings the message, and the main theme finally addresses the Coronavirus directly. Although this date is the 6th Sunday of Easter Vigil, Deacon J. remarks that it does not really feel like the Easter season; it feels more like Lent. The Deacon preaches that we are in need of the Holy Spirit to sustain and strengthen us during this lock-down. In his words, "Catholic people are 'doers' of love, a people of faith and works, and now, during the pandemic, works of love should carry on." This sermon gives new light into the theological view of the pandemic held by "Saint Patty"'s church leadership, that the Holy Spirit is our advocate and helper during the pandemic. According to Father E. and Deacon J., the Holy Spirit is who we should be relying on in this "out-of-order" time, and by His power we can remain faithful in spirit and deed. Deacon J humorously adds that social distancing should not distract believers from the Missio Dei, as it did not deter the disciples. He jokes that the early disciples socially distanced by going out to different places to proclaim the Gospel.

Reflection & the *Missio Dei*

The implicit theological reflections from previous services and the explicit exhortation given by Deacon J. reflect the church's theology of the *Missio Dei* (Mission of God), an understanding that God is powerful and active in the world today and has called His people to share the Good News of the Kingdom of God through word and deed in any circumstance. The church's commitment to praise of God through worship, their willingness to modify sacraments in order for parishioners to participate in those sacred events, and the choice of scriptures, preaching, and prayer indicate the true theology of this parish. Their theology, practiced and lived out, does align with the theology articulated and preached by Father E., Deacon J., and the few parishioners I interviewed. In other words, this parish does what it says it believes.

Father E. described to me his, and the Catholic universal, understanding of suffering, which is the way he is leading his parish to view the pandemic. In Father E.'s understanding, suffering is a by-product of the broken nature of this world. Jesus suffered, the saints of the Catholic faith suffered, and believers too may suffer. The response to this suffering, according to Father E., should be faithful endurance and commitment to the *Missio Dei*. The parish sees themselves as a community set apart and sent out into their community (and the world) to love God and love others, even in the midst of global crisis. Based upon the worshipful attitude of this parish, their work to innovate and modify in order to maintain vital ministries, the commitment to the sacraments they express, and the consistent teaching and bold prayer, one can observe that this faith community believes that God is bigger than COVID-19. They appear to be a church full of people who are willing to faithfully endure suffering and work to participate in the mission of God. Continuing to teach, serve, encourage, send, disciple, praise, rebuke, and celebrate in new and creative ways. Father E. even notes that the pandemic has grown the ministry of "Saint Patty" Church by extending their reach beyond the local area via technology and increased missional impact through giving and using resources, previously unknown to the parish, such as Zoom.

Since "Saint Patty" Catholic Church re-opened its doors on May 25th, parishioners have starting returning and online engagement remains high. The COVID-19 virus persists as a major threat in the United States and Georgia specifically, so the parish will continue in the virtual ministries they began. Email, Facebook, and the church website will continue to be primary vehicles of ministry according to Father E. The church will remain committed to administering the sacraments via online outlets and in-person, following social-distancing guidelines.[5] Father E., Deacon J., and Parishioners L. and K. believe that "Saint Patty"'s ministry will continue for many years to come. They predict that as the COVID-19 virus becomes more controlled in the Middle Georgia area, the people that usually fill the church's seats, lobby, and classrooms will return. Church may be different, perhaps there will be less hugs and handshakes, more health precautions, and ongoing virtual ministries that did not exist before, but the Church will endure this time of suffering as it has for thousands of years.

[5] "Following Governor Kemp's Executive Order: Should My Business Remain Open: Georgia Department of Economic Development." *Following Governor Kemp's Executive Order: Should My Business Remain Open | Georgia Department of Economic Development*, www.georgia.org/covid19bizguide. Retrieved August 10, 2020.

Case Study Three: A People Focused on Victory

Aaron Batey

Aaron began pastoring in Florida 2011. He is currently working on a master's degree at Asbury Theological Seminary. He has been married since 2005 and has two boys.

Context: Coastal Texas
Affiliation: Independent Charismatic
Size: 120-140 attending

Church Context

The Independent Charismatic "Church on the Gulf," is located in a Texas coastal county. Like churches in every part of the world, they are intentionally taking steps to minister to the congregation and community during the pandemic. The county that the church is located in has 830 confirmed cases of COVID-19 as of August 16, 2020, with 32 deaths.[1] The population of the county in 2019 was 36,643.[2] $44,896 is the median household income, with most of the jobs coming from retail, closely followed by construction and healthcare.[3] The population of the county is ethnically diverse, and, according to the leadership team, the congregation reflects the surrounding area, being made up of both Hispanic and non-Hispanic Whites. This can be quickly noticed on a Sunday morning, as the worship team reflects this diversity. The website

[1] Matagorda Regional Medical Center, "COVID-19 Public Information," updated August 16, 2020, accessed August 16, 2020, https://www.matagordaregional.org/covid19

[2] U.S. Census Bureau, "Quick Facts: Matagorda County, Texas," accessed August 16,2020,https://www.census.gov/quickfacts/fact/table/matagordacountytexas/PST045219

[3] Data USA, "Matagorda County, TX," accessed July 20, 2020, https://datausa.io/profile/geo/matagorda-county-tx#economy

also reflects the church's commitment to diversity as you are virtually introduced to the elders and leadership team.

The church is located in a rural part of the county and consistently had an attendance of 120-140 before the pandemic began. In response to recommendations made by the state, the church closed the building to in person worship on March 22nd and remained that way until May 3rd. After reopening the building to congregants, the attendance has ranged from 90-160. The large attendance fluctuation is due, in part, to a vacation Bible school that the church hosted, when they invited the families of the participating young people to join them on a Sunday morning.

The congregation was planted as an independent, nondenominational congregation in 1986 and now has a membership of 50 households. To become a member, you must attend a new member class that is held after a Sunday service, agree with the major beliefs of the church, and believe that God has "planted" you there. After attending the class, a covenant is signed that includes what the member can expect from the church body and what the church body expects from the person. The congregation has been led by three pastors since it was established. Each of the new pastors was raised up from within the congregation.

The congregation has a focus on corporate worship which is evident in their time allotted during a Sunday morning service for worship in song, as well as online offerings throughout the week for the congregation to join in. The style of worship is predominantly contemporary, with a worship team that enjoys multiple vocals, keyboard and piano, electric guitars, bass guitar, and drums. The front of the sanctuary also has a contemporary decor that lacks many of the traditional symbols and fixtures of many traditional mainstream denominations. Although the church has a contemporary feel, the leadership has not introduced stage lighting or effects that lean more towards a concert environment than a traditional worship service.

Church Response

Before the pandemic began, the church had a social media presence, but it was only used to make an occasional announcement. The church also had a website where sermons would be uploaded as podcasts, but no video or livestreaming was done. This is an area where the church grew exponentially during the pandemic. The leadership committed to doing the best possible job of providing virtual worship via livestream as their knowledge and resources could accommodate. Over the course of four weeks, an evolution in the church's ministry can be observed. Sunday morning services from April 12-May 3 were observed and the following paragraphs will note the change in approach over that time period.

April 12, 2020 was Easter Sunday, and this is the fourth Sunday that the congregation had been doing virtual worship services via livestream. It can already be noted that the church is offering not only the regular service, but a link is also offered for the kids to be able to enjoy a special service aimed more towards the younger audience. The church is also utilizing video conferencing technology to host a connect time after the service.

The worship service opens with videos taken at different members' homes of them wishing the church a happy Easter. These members can be seen riding bikes or standing with all of their children. It is one way this otherwise impersonal medium is made to feel more personal and connected. During this portion of the streaming, one of the elders and his wife offers a short encouragement from the comfort of their home.

After these videos, the worship team begins to invite the congregation to join with them from their homes as they lead in songs appropriate for the Easter celebration, including "Forever" by Kari Jobe and "Hallelujah for the Cross" by Chris McClarney. As the time of worship draws to a close, the pastor enters the stage to transition with prayer. It is noteworthy that this seems like a relatively comfortable scene for a group that has only been doing livestreaming for four Sundays.

In the introduction to the sermon, the pastor makes the statement, "Church is empty, but so is the grave." This lets the listener know that

Easter gives us encouragement in what the pastor then refers to as "this season" and "this time." The pastor has a teacher style that brings in many different passages to support the main points in the sermon. The starting text for this Sunday is John 20:19-23. From this text the pastor points out that the disciples celebrated after seeing the risen savior and Jesus offered them peace and the Holy Spirit. The teaching then follows the concept of the Spirit being given for comfort and to offer power to accomplish the mission given by Jesus. The sermon concludes with an encouragement from Hebrews 10:39, "But we are not those who shrink back…" We should celebrate, for He is risen.

This sermon does not have an overwhelming focus on the pandemic. The main theme of the sermon and the worship service in general is on the resurrection and the power of the Holy Spirit now given to the Church to accomplish the Great Commission. This may be because the pastor desires for the congregation to focus on God and the work they are called to do. This is also evident in the encouragement given to focus more on the Word instead of the news. This approach could be equated to a coach making sure the team does not forget the simple fundamentals before a championship game.

Although the pandemic is not mentioned much in the sermon, the church had gone through great lengths to provide connection points for people during the service. The streaming being done in an organic way gives the viewer a familiar feel, even though this may be a different way of experiencing a Sunday morning service. And again, for a church that did not utilize social media before the pandemic, this congregation has done well at adapting quickly to provide opportunities for virtual worship.

The main text for the April 19, 2020 service was Matthew 16:13-16. The message is shaped by the question Jesus asks his disciples: "But who do you say that I am?" The songs that lead up to the sermon included "Unstoppable God" by Elevation Worship and "All Hail King Jesus" by Bethel Music, and they give some answers to this question by worshipping the God that is unstoppable, the king and the fount of living water. The sermon itself is filled once more with many Bible passages that illustrate who Jesus is, both by his words and deeds. The service concludes with the pastor reading Revelation 3:20 and stating that Jesus is knocking on the door of your heart today. If you hear his voice today, let him in. The pastor then leads the listeners in a prayer of confession and faith.

Much like the previous Sunday, this sermon focuses on things that are considered fundamental to the faith. There was not an overwhelming focus on the pandemic, but there are references that acknowledge the reality of how things are different right now. Once again, the pastor uses references to "times like now" to let the listener know that he recognizes things are different. The most specific mention of an effect of the pandemic was a personal reflection on not being able to just go to the store. While these comments do not give a specific theological response to the pandemic, they do let the listener know that the church recognizes the reality of the situation. As the livestream is ending, the pastor says, "We are so excited about what God is doing in this season of the world." While this does not give much direction to the listener, the statement does let the congregation know that God is active "doing" something in the world in the midst of the pandemic.

Between this Sunday and the prior week, it can be noticed that the church is striving even more to reach out to the congregation to keep them connected. The church is providing different links as the stream is beginning. These include slides with instructions with how to get connected and give. They are also promoting more video conference gatherings during the week.

On April 26, one of the elders spoke instead of the pastor. This elder is the founding pastor of the church, and while the current pastor speaks with the voice of a teacher, this particular elder speaks with a prophetic voice. The title of the message is "Where's David?" The speaker begins with a testimony about God speaking to him about the solution to the pandemic. He then uses 1 Samuel 17 to tie the story of David and Goliath to the current situation of the pandemic. The character of Goliath is used by the speaker to illustrate both the pandemic and Satan as the enemy. The elder has a definite opinion on where God stands on the matter of the pandemic. He states that God is not mad at us and "this is not from God." He makes a case for this by saying that Jesus died to pay for our sins, so there is no reason for God to punish us for them again. He then moves to John 10:10 where the thief is described as coming to kill, steal, and destroy. The observation is then made by the speaker that this is what is going on in the pandemic right now.

In the next phase of the message, the speaker moves to the character of David and states that the church needs a David to step forward and fight the enemy with the tools God has given to us. What are those tools the listener may ask? The preacher turns to 2 Chronicles 7:14 to outline the weapons of war:

> and My people who are called by My name humble themselves, and pray and seek My face, and turn from their wicked ways, then I will hear from heaven, and I will forgive their sin and will heal their land. (2 Chronicles 7:14 NASB)

He says that the church is good at praying and seeking God's face, but they need to "get over themselves" and respond with conviction by turning from their wickedness, and then God will heal this land.

The worship for this week went along with the same theme with songs like "See a Victory" by Elevation Worship that sings of victory in Jesus, and that we will see him break down every wall and watch the giants fall. This theme uses imagery from the Old Testament in order to illustrate the victory that God is going to give over the pandemic today.

This week's message presented a contrasting way of addressing the pandemic than can be observed in the previous messages. While the previous message made passing statements to let the listener know that the pastor was not ignorant of the situation, the rest of the sermon could be preached on any other Sunday. This week's message was completely directed toward how the church should view the pandemic and react to it. Even though the speaker for the day is not the pastor and has not been for 12 years, his statements definitely have a noticeable effect on the thinking of the congregation. As can be seen in the next message, it is at least recognized that we have to deal with the statements that were made by the speaker.

May 3 is the first in-person worship with livestreaming still going on. Some changes can be seen in the technology being used as the church continues to adapt and introduce new camera angles and sound.

They are also discussing the latest mandates during the announcements and describing what the church is doing to ensure the safest worship environment possible. The worship began with songs that included "Surrounded" by Upper Room and "In Jesus' Name" by Darlene Zschech that continue to echo the message from the prior week of God delivering His people and setting them free in this present world.

The main text for the sermon was Exodus 13:17-18. The current pastor uses this text to frame his message titled "What are You Doing, God?" The message is about learning the lesson that God is teaching you so that God will move you on to the next place in life. The pastor directly ties the pandemic to something that God is using right now to teach His people. He does not make a definitive statement on whether or not he believes God has caused the pandemic; only that God is using it.

The sermon closes with an encouragement for the congregation to learn what God is teaching them about a new way to "do church" to be able to thrive in relationship with God even if they never have another Sunday morning service. They can do this by practicing good Christianity at home and being in the Word. They should pray for God's will to be done and then "yield to the Spirit."

This message has shown a development in how the pastor addresses the pandemic during his sermons. On Easter and the following Sunday, the application of the text was general and could be applied in a number of different ways. During this week's message, the main points and the application all were pointed toward how the church should respond to the pandemic.

Pastoral Response

While being interviewed, the pastor addressed some of this change in the presentation during the sermons. He stated that at the beginning there seemed to be a lot of divisiveness over the response of the governmental authorities, and he did not want to get involved with that and have the message of the Gospel be hindered, so he walked carefully through the topic as things developed. He stated clearly in the interview that he did not believe that God caused the pandemic, but he does believe that God uses all things. He sees that God has used the pandemic to define more clearly the line between those who trust in Him and those that trust in human beings. He believes that sickness is part of living in a fallen world and can be the "hand of the enemy," but through all of that, God is steadfast, so we can be unwavering in our confidence in God.

One of the most noticeable things that came up while interviewing the pastor was how the pandemic has established his belief that church should be people-focused, as opposed to program-focused. One of the first commitments he made when the in-person services ceased was to personally call all of the families on the membership roster. He then worked with the ministry team to put together groups that would incorporate each of the families so that each leader was responsible for staying in contact with a smaller number of people. These groups used technology like group messaging apps to stay in communication. The pastor was amazed at some of the ministry that came out of the groups, like meals being delivered to people that were in need. People have been stepping up to fill in gaps where they see the need. The culmination of all of this is the vacation Bible school mentioned earlier in this paper. The pastor said that the event was almost completely led by people from the congregation. He believes that it would have gone on without a hitch if he had not been there. This was evidence to him that God is using the pandemic to bring people closer to God and who He wants them to be.

All of this has begun to shape the pastor's vision for the future of the church. He plans on continuing to challenge the people and see how they surprise him with their responses. He also sees the church growing as a multigenerational group where the older voices are heard while they continue to reach out to the younger generation.

All of the people interviewed spoke of the increased commitment of people serving, particularly in the areas of worship and technical support. People that had not previously found a place to serve filled roles in the tech area, and those that were already serving found ways to improve on things they were doing. It can be related to other groups that enter into a stressful situation together, like combat. They find that they have to firm up their commitment to the cause in order for the group to be successful, and this is what each person observed.

Church Response

The people from the congregation that were interviewed were very satisfied with the way that the leadership responded to the pandemic. One of them even went as far as to say he is "100% satisfied." As the pastor noted, the personal calls seemed to be very effective in the church's response. One of the congregants mentioned how much it meant to him that the pastor called him and that he was asked to keep in contact with a few people as well.

The congregants also had a similar view in how they felt the pandemic had shaped their view of God. Both stated that it was not a change in how they viewed God as much as how they viewed worship. One stated that it helped him to remember that worship is a "heart posture." It is about who we worship. The other said that it gave him a greater appreciation for church and worship.

The church used what they described as a tapered approach in reopening. They began with all of the sanctuary set up for social distancing with a special section set aside for those that are at higher risk. Greeters were stationed at a single-entry point with masks and hand sanitizer. The church then split the sanctuary into three areas; one for higher risk, another for social distancing, and a third for those that are not as concerned. It should be noted that all of those interviewed sat in the later section, but it is also noteworthy that one of those interviewed believed that God was uniting the church in how they are dealing with the pandemic and that is a testimony to the general public.

The congregants seemed to listen and apply the messages preached; particularly the last sermon observed. Each one had a different personal way that God was working in them through the pandemic. The first person interviewed discussed how he felt God was softening his heart towards certain social issues. These were things that he had never noticed before, but now he knew that God was working on him to be active in some way. The other interviewee stated that he saw a better focus in himself for seeking God for what is true and a greater boldness. It is interesting the positive effects that each of these people are having on a personal level.

As a whole, each person noted that the congregation seems to be returning to the in-person services with a renewed passion even though they have the option to continue watching the livestream. The pastor noted that there did seem to be a few that had become lax in their relationship to the church, but it was a very small minority. Each of the interviewees expressed their hope that this would be a lasting effect. The pastor stated that he hoped they would never go back to "church as usual," while another of the congregants said that he hoped this was not a "summer camp effect" where people come back all excited and then the passion fades.

While only time can tell what the effects of the pandemic will be, the initial outlook is positive. The tech ministry that has grown so quickly has had a much wider reach than the church originally anticipated, so that is something which they plan to continue to improve on. Another indicator into future impacts is financial trends. This congregation gave generously during the pandemic, so they are not only stable, but can look into the future without trying to catch up from those lost months of revenue.

Reflection & the *Missio Dei*

It was noted earlier that each of the new pastors was called from within the church, so it was already in the character of this congregation to raise up leaders, but the pandemic has shone a light on that characteristic. If the pastor continues to allow people to rise in times of challenge, then this congregation could become known as a church that trains leaders and sends them out.

Of course, there will be those that fall back into their old way of "church as usual," so perhaps the new groups that the leadership has put into place can help to encourage those that become lax or lose focus. These groups could also be a mechanism for many other types of ministries within the church or new church plants as they are sent out as core groups to reach new communities. Much like the cell group model that is used in different parts of the world, this adds a depth in leadership that is not present when it is only the pastor trying to lead a group of people by themself.

I have been acquainted with this church and its ministries for about seven years now and have known them to be a young and vibrant group in comparison to the average group of church leaders. I have hosted the former pastor for a week at my home and stayed with the current pastor during a week-long retreat for ministers, so I consider both of them friends and people that can hold me accountable in ministry. I have never met the elder that is the founding pastor of the church, and it was not until a few months ago that the current pastor mentioned to me that he was excited to have him commit to supporting the ministry in a greater way through teaching and mentoring. I can see through the elder's prophetic teaching that it is important to have a person that will open that door of proclamation so that others can walk through it. To stick with the illustration he used, he was the David that stepped forward and the Israelites then followed into the battle.

To reflect on that point a little deeper, the teaching that directly addressed the current situation the congregation was facing set the tone and direction that the following sermon and applications followed. This shows how important it is to boldly yet cautiously approach such issues. We can see from the current state of the church in the United States that it is not always the first or loudest voices that need to be followed, so this shows the need for prophetic voices that can discern the times and speak the truth.

As I think about how this church fits into the *Missio Dei*, I cannot help but think about how some of their position comes from the Charismatic DNA that they were birthed with. They already have a view that God is working everywhere and is present in every part of people's lives. This is what Paul G. Hiebert wrote about in his article, "The Flaw of the Excluded Middle."[4] There is a place between the empirical material world and the lofty theology that addresses heaven and eternity, and that in-between he calls the "excluded middle." It is where everyday life is affected by spiritual beings. Many Charismatic churches, including this one, do not exclude this from their theology. They believe that there are spiritual forces at work in their everyday life; they just need to know the biblical answers to what is going on. That is why the last observed sermon from the pastor was so important. For a faith tradition that does

[4] Gallagher, R. L., & Hertig, P. (2009). *Landmark Essays in Mission and World Christianity*. Orbis.

not neglect the spiritual in their everyday life, they needed to hear what God was doing right now, and how to respond.

In shaping this response, the pastor's continual encouragement for the people to spend more time in the Word is very important. As Christopher J. H. Wright put it:

> This is the story that we need to know that we are part of. For our mission is nothing less (or more) than participating with God in the grand story until He brings it to its guaranteed climax.[5]

The people can then begin to understand that they are the Church that is sent by God in much the same way that their membership covenant states that it is God that has "planted" them in that congregation. They are part of that story that they read about on the pages. This view is also evident in the use of Old Testament illustrations such as David and Goliath and the call for people to be not just like David, but to be "a David." This helps to reinforce the teaching that they are part of the grand story that is playing out in the Bible.

As the pastor was discussing the future direction of the church, he said that two things will affect it. The first was future governmental mandates. The church followed the first recommendations as a way of honoring the authority that God has placed there, and he planned to continue to honor that as long as the Gospel could still go forth. The other, more important, factor he referred to as the divine mandates. This included the church's response to the commands of God and what He was doing in shaping them through the pandemic. This illustrates once more that the leadership and environment within this church is one that understands the *Missio Dei*. They are waiting to be directed on this mission as an army is trained and then sent on a directive.

The concept of this church being in prophetic dialogue is the most prominent theme that can be observed through the services and interviews. As Bevans and Schroeder point out in their book *Prophetic Dialogue*, reaching out into a new culture requires dialogue with the

5 Wright, Christopher J. H., *The Mission of God's People* (Zondervan, 2010), 44.

culture, but it also has a place for a prophetic voice as well.[6] Although this church is not moving into a new culture, they are reaching out into a new situation within their home culture. You can see the time of dialogue that the pastor goes through as he discerns the divisiveness that is being caused, and he is careful not to jump hastily and cause harm to the ministry of the church. The prophetic voice of the more-experienced elder then steps in and calls for action and sets a direction for the people. This has an effect that sets the course of the congregation, both lay and leadership alike, that will continue to steer the church in the near future and possibly much longer.

---

[6] Bevan, Stephen B., Schroeder, Roger. *Prophetic Dialogue: Reflections on Christian Mission Today* (Maryknoll, NY: Orbis 2001).

Case Study Four: Socially Distancing, but Not Spiritually Distancing

Lindsey L. Croston

Lindsey L. Croston is an ordained minister with the Assemblies of God. She serves as a faculty member in the Barnett College of Ministry and Theology at Southeastern University in Central Florida. She is passionate about teaching students how to connect with the biblical narrative and God's mission in the world.

Context: Suburban Central Florida
Affiliation: Assemblies of God
Size: 1,200-2,500+ in attendance

Church Context

"Avenue" Church is a large (2500+ attendees) church in a suburban city in Central Florida. It is located between two metropolitan areas (less than a one hour drive). The church began as a small group in the senior pastor's living room 13 years ago. From there it became a non-denominational church meeting in a local high school. In 2019, the church joined the Assemblies of God (A/G) and the pastor was ordained with that fellowship. In the words of the senior pastor, Pastor Jeremy, "we don't really do membership,"[1] but the weekly services before the pandemic averaged around 1200 attendees. Before the pandemic, the church was renting space from a local high school in the southern section of the city, which has a higher socioeconomic bracket than the rest of the city. Its attendees vary in age, but the majority of attendees fall in the 30-50 age bracket, and many of them are younger families. The senior pastor described their worship service as "modern," because the

---

1 Phone interview with senior pastor, July 21, 2020.

term “contemporary” felt dated. It has a Charismatic tendency and the worship team plays a lot of Bethel and Elevation songs.

The pandemic had a relatively low outbreak in the area near the beginning of March, but the “shut down” of various counties in the state began in mid-March. The governor issued an official “safer-at-home” order beginning April 3 and lasting through April 30.[2] The county where the church is located originally had lower cases of Coronavirus-19 than the two metropolitan areas surrounding it, but as the state began to open in May, the county became a hotspot for cases, averaging 7-10% higher infection rates than the rest of the state.[3] Area schools closed a week before their scheduled spring break in mid-March, and remained closed for the rest of the school year (beginning remote education at the beginning of April). Since the church meets in a school, they found out on Friday, March 13, 2020 that they would not be able to have services in the building that Sunday, March 15, 2020. Pastor Jeremy noted that their staff had to “scramble” to get a message put together and pre-recorded for that Sunday, since they would be unable to meet face-to-face with their congregation.

Since the decision to move to strictly online was made for them, Pastor Jeremy said the question then became how to approach the different guidelines that were coming down from local, state, and national leaders. Two weeks before Easter Sunday, the “safer-at-home” measure went into effect, and so the staff pulled together two online services, pre-recording several worship sets so they could have a full band for streamed worship before the rules for gathering went into effect. One thing the staff was particularly focused on was being “socially conscious.” Pastor Jeremy noted, “The state said ‘no gatherings of more than 10 people,’ but somehow churches were exempt from that? It didn’t make sense to us, so we focused on being a good neighbor to our community and following group guidelines.” Pastor Jeremy was especially concerned with trying not to do anything that would “misrepresent us or our hearts” at “Avenue” Church.

---

[2] WFTS Digital Staff, “Gov. DeSantis Signs Safer-at-Home Order,” *WFTS ABC Action News*, April 1, 2020. Accessed August 13, 2020. https://www.abcactionnews.com/news/coronavirus/gov-desantis-signs-safer-at-home-order-directing-residents-to-limit-movements-to-essential-activities.

[3] Florida Covid-19 Dashboard, Accessed August 10, 2020. https://experience.arcgis.com/experience/96dd742462124fa0b38ddedb9b25e429.

Congregational Response & Social Media

The church already streamed services live on Sundays before the pandemic began. However, the short notice of schools closing caused some temporary hurdles for their staff. The church had begun a sermon series on relationships the Sunday before things started shutting down, and quickly shifted to a new series titled, "Hope." The first "pandemic" sermon was posted for the Sunday, March 15 service and was a short, 12-minute sermon with Pastor Jeremy titled, "Not Afraid – Fear, Faith, and Trapeze."

As the state issued a lock-down, the church staff at first was scrambling to put together ideas for how to connect online with their people outside of the Sunday morning service stream. They scheduled "stripped down worship Wednesdays" on Facebook Live with the Worship Pastor (Alex) and other worship team members. Pastor Jeremy and his wife Emma hosted Monday night prayer on Facebook and Instagram Live, rebroadcast popular messages for a "Throwback Thursday," and even hosted online Friday night game nights. In Pastor Jeremy's words, "We felt the need to be there 24/7." Now the staff conversation is focused more on how to interact with people throughout the week long-term without feeling like they need to host 4-5 "live" events per week.

One thing that specifically changed in the church's online ministry platform during the pandemic was having staff online in the chat areas during the "normal" service times, trying to facilitate conversations among those who were watching. It was something that the church had not done previously, since all the staff were engaged in face-to-face ministry on Sunday mornings.

For the four weeks that were specifically studied, the church wrapped up its "Hope" series on April 12, 2020 with an Easter Sunday message titled "3 Days to Hope," and then launched a new series titled "New Normal" that began April 19, 2020 and ran through May 3, 2020. By the May 3 service, the state's "lockdown" orders were lifted, and the state entered its "Phase 1" plan of reopening. Schools were still closed, so the church remained an "online-only" presence. As of August 15, 2020, "Avenue" Church has not resumed face-to-face services, and with their building project behind schedule due to pandemic-related delays, Pastor

Jeremy does not think they will meet together for a "normal" worship service until the beginning of 2021. However, there are some plans to meet at a different facility on a monthly basis until the new building is ready to open.

April 12, 2020

This Sunday's message was titled "3 Days to Hope." It focused on the celebration of Easter Sunday. The video service began with an online countdown showcasing photos submitted or tagged in the church's social media of families watching from home, as well as messages about upcoming "Next Steps" classes, ways to be connected, options for giving, and the "live chat" during the message for normal service times. The youth pastor, Isaac (a young African American male), and children's pastor, Iris (middle-aged non-white female) opened the service with a pre-recorded welcome, addressing the "remote" situation and emphasized how to interact in the chat, encouraging congregants to share the message, and giving a few reminders of elements that were in the pre-service slides. Pastor Alex and a medium-sized band (piano, 2 acoustic guitars, an electric guitar, drums, and 3 vocalists (including the Worship Pastor) led worship. The songs were "God so Loved" by We the Kingdom Music and "Resurrecting" by Elevation Worship. A video montage of congregation members sharing what their life was like before Jesus followed, with each person ending their clip with the phrase, "hope has a name." The montage showed a diverse group of members – males, females, and a range of ages and ethnicities.

After the video montage, the senior pastor greeted the congregation, and taught them the traditional liturgical phrase for Easter, "The Lord is risen – he is risen indeed." His message used texts from Romans 8:11, 23 and John 11:25-26. Pastor Jeremy talked about the three days of Easter: Friday is the day of pain, Saturday is the day of confusion, Sunday is the day of resurrection. He focused on God's presence and purpose in each of those days, and while the pandemic was not referenced specifically, there were several side comments that acknowledged the realities and fears that congregants might be facing. A phrase that was used repeatedly by various staff members was "socially distancing, but not spiritually distancing." Pastor Jeremy reminded the congregation: "there is no pain that his purpose can't redeem" and "there is no confusion that his presence cannot calm." This sermon wrapped up the series on Hope that the church had been working through since the pandemic closures began. The pastor closed with an invitation for salvation, and an encouragement to connect with the church if a decision to follow Christ was made, and the worship band closed out the service with "Hope Has a Name" by River Valley Worship.

April 19, 2020

This week began a new series titled "New Normal." The same opening slides from the previous week were utilized, with updated photos from social media posts. A similar band (different vocalist, less guitars) opened the service after a greeting from the youth pastor, recording from his living room. Between the worship set and the sermon was a testimony clip from a homeless ministry the church had supported in the recent weeks. The "homeless pastor" shared how the homeless population in the city was facing a high level of dehydration because public spaces where they would normally go to cool off and get free water were closed due to the pandemic. A donation from the church allowed the ministry to purchase water at cost from some water companies and between 500-750 homeless individuals were able to receive water daily.

Pastor Jeremy brings this week's message from his living room. The title was "A New Identity," and it ties together last week's message on Easter Sunday and the new series, "New Normal." The scripture passages used were Ephesians 2:1-10 and John 20:19, 10:10. In this message, the pastor opened sharing some examples of how life has changed since the pandemic began, and some of the challenges faced (e.g. cutting his own hair), as well as the blessings of a slower pace and spending more time with family. While Pastor Jeremy did not specifically address a theological understanding of the pandemic, the underlying theme of hope continues from the week before, and a focus on finding identity in Christ instead of in circumstances shape the expected response of the congregation to the difficulties they are facing. Themes of trust and thankfulness that began in the worship set are carried through to the sermon and personal examples given within the message.

April 26, 2020

This week is the second week in the "New Normal" series. Again, the video opens with slide reminders and photos, and a welcome message is brought from the children's pastor, filmed in her living room. A similar band from previous weeks leads worship, and the songs are "Great Things" and "Living Hope," both by Phil Wickham. Between the worship set and the message, a video from a missionary in Fiji is shared. The missionary is good friends with Pastor Jeremy, and he shares what the pandemic is like in Fiji and how the church's generous donation has allowed him and his family to minister to those around them.

The title of this week's message is "Wholeness," and it continues to build on last week's themes. This time the focus is on healing and restoration, and changing from "how it was to how it needs to be." Pastor Jeremy shapes the pandemic as an opportunity for people to "change course," to trust God and find identity within him, not in the circumstances people find themselves in. While he doesn't specifically mention the pandemic, there are several general references to things being different and challenges that people are facing. The focus is consistently on finding hope in God and living the lives God has called us to live. His illustrations in this week's message are broad, ranging from Michelangelo's Pieta, to Humpty Dumpty, to the Power Rangers (as a connection to the Greek word metamorphoo). Consistent reminders to replace worry and fear with trust in God are peppered throughout the message.

May 3, 2020

This Sunday marks eight weeks of online-only services for "Avenue" Church. In some of his opening remarks, Pastor Jeremy notes how he misses several different things and how he is thankful for some things, and asks for online interaction of congregants to share what they are thankful for and what they miss about "normal" life. This week's title is "Heart and Soul" and it is the conclusion for the "New Normal" series. Staff member Terrie, who is the "Team Avenue Coach and Outreach Coordinator," brings the welcome message. She brings some specific announcements, but there are no "announcement slides" or "countdown" this week. The worship band sings "God of Miracles" by Chris McClarney and "Waymaker" by Osinachi Kalu Okoro Egbu.

The message text this week is 1 Samuel 14:1-15, and Hebrews 10:25 and Proverbs 21:5 are also referenced. While the pandemic is still not specifically mentioned, there are again comments on the discouragement that many are facing, and that the church needs to continue ministering even in different circumstances. He talks about how the world "accelerates and accentuates fear" and the need for community ("godly inspiration requires collaboration, which cannot happen in isolation"). The overall theme continues to be that God is in control, and that the Church's response needs to be one of hope, faith, trust, and encouragement.

The online presence during these four weeks was consistently frank about realities without getting bogged down in details. While the pandemic was rarely specifically identified (possibly because it was addressed in previous sermons before this four-week period), the situations and struggles that people were facing were acknowledged. The overall tone of worship sets, messages, welcome messages, and other communication was one of hope and encouragement. The variety and diversity of staff highlighted showcases what kind of church "Avenue" is on a regular basis. At one point during this four-week period, the senior pastor was supposed to graduate with his Doctor of Ministry degree, and the congregation slipped in a "congratulations" video montage to support their pastor. Sermons were conversational in tone (which was the style before the pandemic as well). Youth and children's ministries had an online presence as well, and the church's website had a link to "parent resources" prominently displayed. The responsibility of church members to be "good neighbors" and to support community authority was emphasized without being overbearing. A consistent message of the church's mission ("we exist to help people take the next step in their relationship with Jesus") and the culture of generosity is communicated in each service.

Pastoral Response

An interview with Pastor Jeremy provided some insights into the challenges of leading a church in the midst of a pandemic. The challenges of not owning the location where they meet have created some unique issues for this church. They were meeting at a high school, but since the schools shut down, they have been fully online. While schools are reopening for students in late August, they are not open for outside rentals. As a result, the pastoral staff has been working with another church to use their building once a month (beginning at the end of August) for monthly worship services. The rest of their ministries are still happening online or in small groups.

Pastor Jeremy emphasized repeatedly that just because the building was closed did not mean the church had shut down. There were new needs, and different problems to tackle, but ministry was still happening. One of the unexpected side effects of moving to online-only was that there was less to talk about throughout the week on social media. Since they were not having their traditional services, there was no way to get pictures that would then boost their social media posts throughout the week. The church has done several different things to keep people engaged without traditional services. They hosted an online VBS, and sent out "home bags" to the children who were already a part of the ministry full of supplies for the event. The children's pastor organized some parades past kids' homes (particularly for birthdays and "graduating" fifth graders). The church has done a lot of "need-meeting" for congregants: they paid bills, helped people through different situations that resulted from the pandemic, and have continued to give generously to the community and global partners. They hosted a "single mom car checkup" in April, which was something they already did on a regular basis before the pandemic. Single moms could sign up for appointments on the church's website, and they brought their cars in for a simple "checkup" and oil change. The youth group washed the cars for the moms, and the church provided coffee and breakfast from a local coffee shop in the location where the event was hosted. For this particular event during the pandemic, about 15-20 moms signed up. Another challenge that the church has faced due to the pandemic is that a lot of the organizations they partner with in the community are closed to volunteers for the time being. As a result, the staff have had to approach community service in different ways. In the later part of the summer, the church asked teachers within the congregation to provide Amazon wish lists for their classrooms, and encouraged the church to help meet those needs.

Overall, Pastor Jeremy observed that the church was seeing their core people stay connected, and the "fringe" attenders were popping in and out as it was convenient for them. They still saw a full range of participants, just in smaller numbers. Other pastors he has connected with are saying that a certain percentage of pre-Covid attendance has dropped since they have reopened. For this area, that may be because the case numbers are still going up, but Pastor Jeremy also noted that it might be because it "feels weird to go back to church under new circumstances." Normally, they have around 5,000-plus views of their online services a weekend, but there is no way to know how long those views lasted (did they watch for a little bit and drop out, or did they watch the whole service?). The total engagement (including people who watch services later in the week) has stayed "pretty solid", but the live engagement has dropped post-Easter. Pastor Jeremy cited Craig Groeschel, who is one of the pioneers of the church online platform, saying that Groeschel's ministry noted that churches who opened up early where they were able saw a spike around Easter in engagement and then that "fell off a cliff" after. "Avenue" Church has had a similar experience: their numbers were high for Easter, but then they dropped off significantly. At the time of the interview (June 2020), the numbers seemed to have settled for them.

When asked about his theological approach to the pandemic, Pastor Jeremy started his response by referencing the prophet Isaiah. In the King James Version, Isaiah 6:1 states, "In the year King Uzziah died, I also saw the Lord." Pastor Jeremy noted that "so often for us, time has this way of marking us – remembering where you were on 9/11, when you proposed, etc. We mark time in moments." In his opinion, the pandemic is one of those "moments." The passage from Isaiah is pertinent because Uzziah dying was a tragedy, but at the same time, Isaiah saw the Lord, which meant God was not absent. As followers of Jesus, believers are also able to see God's work at play in situations, and to realize that we have a hope the rest of the world doesn't have.

"The reality is, we live in a broken, fallen world. This was never God's intention, but God is still at work" in the middle of that brokenness. Pastor Jeremy sees the pandemic as one of the greatest opportunities for the Church as a whole, and referenced Acts as an example of what he meant. "In the book of Acts, if you zoom out, you see this situation where Jesus leaves, and the Holy Spirit comes, and the Church explodes, but stays centered in Jerusalem. Then, great persecution breaks out, and the Church spreads out. In some way, we could zoom out of this story and see the church was doing good at having services, but then the church had to decentralize because of the pandemic." As a result, the church is now meeting in many different locations, both face-to-face and virtually. Now there is an opportunity for people who might not have come before to a church building to experience and participate in church in different ways.

Throughout the services observed for this project, Pastor Jeremy's consistent approach to the situation faced by his congregants is one of hope and trust. From the worship sets to the examples given in the sermon, the message of "God is bigger than this" comes through clearly. There were no "doom and gloom" messages, or even messages that were focused on eternity during this time period. The theological message proffered by "Avenue" Church during the pandemic is full of hope and encouragement. It does not deny the reality of the situation, or downplay its significance, but the congregation is encouraged to find its identity in something greater than their circumstances. They are frequently reminded that there are others who need help, and that through their generosity, those needs are being met. The staff lives out the church's tagline: "We exist to help you take the next step in your relationship with Jesus" by encouraging congregants to continue pursuing their faith and to connect with one another in new ways. Something staff members said repeatedly in various services was the phrase, "Just because we're socially distancing doesn't mean we are spiritually distant." The view of the Church as more than a building and the purpose of the Church to minister to those around them remained a key characteristic of "Avenue" Church during the pandemic.

Congregational Response

From formal and informal interviews conducted with congregants, the congregation seems to be connecting well with the message that Pastor Jeremy and the staff are communicating. Two formal interviews with congregants were conducted in addition to the interview with Pastor Jeremy, and observations were made based on casual conversations with other church members.

The first formal interview was with Rebecca, who is a Caucasian female in her mid-late 30s.[4] She noted that she had not watched every week's sermon, but part of that was because her husband is on staff and so she knew already what the sermon topic was each week and they process that throughout the week as a family. She had watched some services of other churches, but that was partly because they were able to see friends who are ministry leaders elsewhere. She specifically mentioned missing the face-to-face element of worship. "There's something so special about coming together with others pointing to Jesus with their words and songs." At the same time, while she plans to attend once face-to-face services resume, the one thing she is unsure of is whether her kids will attend the children's services right away. She would feel comfortable having them with her in a main service, but possibly not in kids' church. Rebecca noted that some of the biggest changes once "Avenue" returns to face-to-face services is that there will be a lot of people who won't be back because they have had to move and take jobs in other areas of the state/country. At the same time, she noted that there were many people who they had been inviting to church who had been attending online services, so there might be a lot of new faces once traditional services resume. She anticipates the church will continue to have online services and connections on Sundays.

Rebecca's theological approach to the pandemic is perhaps a unique one. Approximately five years ago, her oldest son passed away. (He was severely disabled, and had lived much longer than anyone expected him to when he was born.) In reflecting on the pandemic, Rebecca drew on her previous experiences to help shape her theological perspective. "For us, personally, when you walk through a time when you're very much out of control, there's a lot of laying down and surrendering [the

[4] Phone interview, July 24, 2020.

situation] back to the Lord and trusting that He is still with us and still in control. I'm in control of my response, He's in charge." While the pandemic didn't affect her view of God, it did help her to return to this place of surrender and trust quickly, because it was another "out of control situation." As a family, they focused on worship to refocus and get their minds off the immediate and shift their perspective to what God would have them focus on.

Overall, Rebecca felt that the church had done a good job of responding to the pandemic situation. "Pastor Jeremy jumps at a challenge. He and his wife both – it's quick and in a slightly thriving way – they appreciate a challenge and approach it as doing their best." She also felt like the children's ministry had done a good job at reaching out to her daughters during this time, who had received handwritten postcards from leaders.

The second formal interview was with Terri, an African American female in her early-mid 30s. She also had a very positive response when questioned about how "Avenue" Church had approached the pandemic. She felt like the pastoral staff had managed the situation "with creativity and grace."[5] Her family has kept up with most of the services online and enjoy that way of being connected. At the same time, they miss the community and live worship setting. She mentioned that her sons particularly missed kids' church. However, "the quality of church hasn't been diminished. It's been neat seeing how creative our church has been during this time." She remarked that the church's leadership had been excellent at keeping them in community, despite social distancing protocols.

Terri's theological response to the pandemic was less nuanced than Rebecca's, but it still carried the overall themes that Pastor Jeremy's messages had communicated. Terri noted that God "is still good and still fully in control," so she didn't think that God's role in the world had been affected by the pandemic. She observed that the pandemic had reminded her that "time on earth is fleeting," which helped her to refocus on her purpose to lead people to Christ and to be more "dialed in" at home.

---

[5] Interview via Facebook Messenger, July 27, 2020.

Overall, "Avenue"'s approach to the pandemic has reflected the church's bigger mission and purpose: connecting others to growth in a personal relationship with Christ. This has been achieved through many smaller actions and consistent teaching and modeling by leadership.

Post-Pandemic Future

The pandemic continues to affect the congregation of "Avenue" Church, well beyond the scope of this study. Their experience has perhaps been longer than other churches', due to their unique situation of renting their property instead of owning it. Beyond the initial impact of service locations, however, both Pastor Jeremy and the two congregants interviewed identified potential impacts of the pandemic on "Avenue" Church as a whole.

The potential impacts predicted by the congregants were straightforward. Rebecca noted that the people of "Avenue" Church would be different once face-to-face services resumed. This was both a positive and a negative change. Positive, because she anticipated people who had connected with the church during the pandemic online would join in face-to-face events, and negative because the church had lost some of its regular attenders because of Covid-related job losses. She also opined that the church would likely retain some sort of interactive feature on their livestream, since it had become an essential part of services during this period. Terri observed that she did not anticipate too many changes to the church once traditional services resumed. She thought they might increase their online presence, but did not think much more than that would be necessary.

Pastor Jeremy's discussion of future impacts was more detailed and focused on both individual and community needs. When asked about the long-term effects the pandemic might have on the church, he opened his response by stating, "We don't know what normal is going to look like, so there are a lot of unknowns." Some of the big challenges he anticipates facing include mental health issues, financial needs, and health needs. He anticipates that the church will need to be more proactive in sharing how they are working to keep people healthy and safe. He also anticipates that mental health issues will begin to skyrocket at the end of 2020 and beginning of 2021. Overall, though, the real ministry of the church will not be impacted. "Ministry was not about church services; it was about reaching people. The service was just the vehicle." While that vehicle will likely change shape, and Pastor Jeremy anticipates adding additional staff to continue the interactive nature of their online presence once traditional services resume, it was clear from our interactions that the mission of "Avenue" Church would remain the same.

Reflection & the *Missio Dei*

I found "Avenue" Church's approach to the pandemic to be refreshing and encouraging. The consistency of their presentation, the conversational tone of their services, and the energy of the worship team all combined to create an overall presence that strengthened the message being preached. While the church is made up of varying age groups, the majority of the demographic is families with the parents in their 30s and 40s. The approach that the pastoral staff takes to ministry seems to fit this demographic well. The issues that were addressed met felt needs of young families facing uncertain times in the face of the pandemic.

The church does a good job of communicating their mission and vision, and in providing opportunities for individuals to connect with staff. There were small groups that met both virtually and (once the state had lifted its stay-at-home orders) in homes. The highlights of ways the church was making tangible differences in the community and with global partners helped viewers/congregants to see how ministry was continuing even in the midst of the pandemic. The church's commitment to honoring civil leaders and their consistent communication of how the actions they were choosing were intentional in providing a witness to the larger community was refreshing in the midst of the polemic narrative of the media.

"Avenue" Church understands at a molecular level what *Missio Dei* is about. They are devoted to blessing not only their constituency, but their community, and even the world, through their message and generosity. Each online service ended with an invitation to begin a relationship with Jesus, and the opportunity to connect with pastoral staff in several ways to communicate that commitment. Beyond that, a "Next Steps" class was available "on demand" for people to find out the mission and vision of the church and how they could fit into that partnership. A second level of the "Next Steps" class, which focuses on spiritual gifts and discipleship was held through Zoom during the pandemic. Their mission, "to help people take the next step in their relationship with Jesus" is an excellent summary of what *Missio Dei* is, and how it can be lived out in local community.

Case Study Five: Looking for God's Good in Life's Circumstances

Valerie Walker

Valerie Walker lives in Houston, Texas, where she teaches MBA students at her alma mater, Rice University, and has been engineer for the energy industry for over 15 years, after graduating from Texas A&M University with a BS in Mechanical Engineering. Valerie is pursuing a MA in Biblical Studies at Asbury and enjoys running with her chocolate lab, live music, painting, and spending time with her family.

Context: Suburban, Texas
Affiliation: United Methodist
Size: 13,000 members

Church Context

The church that was observed during the pandemic was the "Methodome" United Methodist Church located in the suburbs of a major city in Texas. It has approximately 13,000 members and has around 1,500 people that worship at its traditional service on any given Sunday. This suburb was heavily impacted by Covid-19. The Texas governor announced the closure of schools, bars, restaurants and gyms on March 20,2020.[1] The particular suburb where the "Methodome" United Methodist Church is located was hit especially hard by the disease and the county issued stay at home orders March 27, 2020. The orders were lifted on April 17, 2020. Since then, the county has had cycles of spikes in the number of Covid-19 cases throughout the summer and reached the highest number of cases to date in late summer of 2020.

[1] https://gov.texas.gov/news/post/governor-abbott-issues-executive-orders-to-mitigate-spread-of-covid-19-in-texas

Church Response & Social Media

The "Methodome" United Methodist Church had a strong social media presence before the Covid-19 outbreak. They even have a large bank of sermons stored on an online library on the church's website. The church stopped having services in-person midweek March 8, 2020, trying to help stop the spread of the virus in the local area. Four sermons during the pandemic time period, April 12th, 19th, 26th, and May 3 were analyzed. All four of these services were only conducted online and only had the staff present in the sanctuary.

There was no music recorded in the service archives. Only the sermon was recorded. The sermon online archive was difficult to find to watch the videos from the main church homepage, and they were not organized by date, but, rather, by series. This service, in particular, was attended by a more elderly population. One would assume finding the online archive would be especially difficult for them.

Dr. Sam gave the sermon for the April 12th Easter Sunday service. The son of a pastor, he started the "Methodome" United Methodist Church in 1978, and has served there since as the head pastor, which is not common in the United Methodist denomination. Dr. Sam is an older Caucasian gentleman with parted grey hair, married, and has seven grandchildren.

The pastor's attire was white robes with a pink designed sash. There were candles, beautiful pink floral arrangements, and white Easter lilies by the pulpit, along with a soft, purple, glowing light at the altar from stain glass windows in the background. The pastor spoke boldly, slowly, and clearly, as if he was making a speech to a live audience, and he used a small microphone, even though no one was there in the sanctuary except the staff. Specific verses the pastor quoted were shown in the text at the bottom of the screen when read.

The scripture used for the April 12th service was the Luke 24:13-35, which covers the story of some followers of Jesus, who were discussing Jesus's crucifixion while traveling to Emmaus. Jesus joins the followers on their travels and the men do not recognize him until he joins them as a host for dinner. At this time, they praised him, believed in his resurrection, and went to share the good news with others. Romans 8:28 was also referenced in the sermon by Dr. Sam: "*And we know that in all things God works for the good of those who love him, who have been called according to his purpose.*"

The main theme of the sermon emphasized that bad circumstances, specifically the Corona virus, can be used by God for good. In fact, the whole sermon was about awful circumstances that God ended up using for good. Dr. Sam relates the pandemic experience to the scripture passage by stating the men walking to Emmaus were discussing the sad situation of Jesus's death when Jesus engaged them. In their lowest, most desperate time, God was with them. Dr. Sam noted that when Jesus hosted them for dinner, that is when their eyes were opened. Dr. Sam enthusiastically announced this is the same case in the pandemic!

He stressed the congregation needs to be looking for God, who is already with us, in any situation. God is working for good in every circumstance, even ones where hope seems to be lost. God showed how the horrible circumstance of Jesus's crucifixion led to the goodness of Christ's resurrection.

Dr. Sam further encouraged the congregation to respond to the pandemic by having faith that God will use this bad circumstance to bring good. He challenged the congregation multiple times to look for the good that God is already doing during this pandemic. Dr. Sam even started the sermon by pointing out the difference in this particular Easter worship, which was not being attended in person. He encouraged everyone to acknowledge the situation, that he has experienced the same, and that none of them wanted these circumstances. Dr. Sam talked about the Spanish influenza and how City Methodist Hospital nurses worked to help heal people during that time, and they can do the same now with this pandemic.

Dr. Sam's theological view of the pandemic from the angle of this sermon is that God can use the pandemic to create good. God loves us and doesn't want bad things for us. At the same time, we live in the broken world, full of sin and awful things, such as the pandemic, which is why God sent Jesus to save us.

Dr. Sam also gave the sermon for the April 19th service. This time the pastor's attire was black robes with a yellow designed sash. There were candles by the pulpit with stain glass windows in the background. Again, the pastor spoke boldly, slowly and clearly as if he was making a speech to an audience with a microphone even though no one was in the sanctuary except the staff.

Matthew 11:28-30, Isaiah 61:3, and John 21:15 were used as the scripture text for this sermon. Matthew 11 reads: "*Come to me, all you who are weary and burdened, and I will give you rest. 29 Take my yoke upon you and learn from me, for I am gentle and humble in heart, and you will find rest for your souls. 30 For my yoke is easy and my burden is light." Isaiah 61:3 records, "and provide for those who grieve in Zion to bestow on them a crown of beauty instead of ashes, the oil of joy instead of mourning, and a garment of praise instead of a spirit of despair. They will be called oaks of righteousness, a planting of the LORD for the display of his splendor." While John 21:15 notes, "When they had finished eating, Jesus said to Simon Peter, 'Simon son of John, do you love me more than these?' 'Yes, Lord,' he said, 'you know that I love you.' Jesus said, 'Feed my lambs.'"*

The main theme of the sermon was making peace with the past. Dr. Sam discusses bringing past wounds to Jesus and let him, the Great Physician, heal you. He also adds to repent and turn to God to seek forgiveness of God to be free of your sin. He did not directly tie the text to the Corona Virus pandemic in this sermon; however, the healing and physician reference give an indirect tie to the pandemic. Dr. Sam did start the sermon reflecting again how Easter was different this year, due to the pandemic.

The April 26th sermon was given by a bishop who has been in ministry for over 40 years. He preaches at some of the traditional services and advises the other "Methodome" United Methodist Church pastors. He is an older African American gentleman with grey combed hair and glasses. He is married and has 2 grandchildren. The bishop wore a black robe with a yellow designed sash.

The scripture text used by the bishop was 2 Corinthians 12:7-8: "*…or because of these surpassingly great revelations. Therefore, in order* *to keep me from becoming conceited, I was given a thorn in my flesh, a messenger of Satan, to torment me. [8] Three times I pleaded with the Lord to take it away from me."* Another scripture for this sermon used was Philippians 4:11-13, *"[11] I am not saying this because I am in need, for I have learned to be content whatever the circumstances. [12] I know what it is to be in need, and I know what it is to have plenty. I have learned the secret of being content in any and every situation, whether well fed or hungry, whether living in plenty or in want. [13] I can do all this through him who gives me strength."*

This sermon was a part of a sermon series called "Making Peace," specifically with our circumstances. The bishop stated the pastors had planned this series and sermon much earlier, before the pandemic, but it turned out to be quite timely. The bishop's theological view of the pandemic seemed to be in line with Dr. Sam. He stated the congregation should be content with circumstances, which can only be found with strength through Christ. The bishop acknowledged people who are struggling with real life issues due to the pandemic, such as the loss of a job. He encouraged the congregation not to attempt handling the circumstances by themselves, but, rather, to put our hope and trust in God.

The Bishop began the sermon by stating the congregation had been in quarantine for six weeks. He also stated that everyone used to desire to be home; now, we want to go out! There were candles and a metal cross by the pulpit, with stain glass windows in the background. The bishop also spoke boldly, slowly and clearly as if he was making a speech to an audience with a microphone, just like Dr. Sam.

Dr. Sam returned to preach the May 3rd sermon. The scripture text used was Matthew 5:9 "*Blessed are the peacemakers, for they will be called children of God;*" and also Matthew 5:23-24, "*Therefore, if you are offering your gift at the altar and there remember that your brother or sister has something against you, [24] leave your gift there in front of the altar. First go and be reconciled to them; then come and offer your gift.*"

The main theme of the sermon, also from the series "Making Peace," addressed specifically dealing with our enemies. Dr. Sam tied the text to the Corona-virus pandemic by referring to conflicts in homes between family members during the pandemic. He also referred to another conflict between a business owner and an employee during another pandemic. He then encouraged the congregation to extend grace and reconciliation. The pastor mentioned at the beginning of the sermon that attendance is the same online as in-person. He also mentioned that services will continue like this for a while.

Pastoral Approach

Reverend Jennifer works with Dr. Sam and the bishop, and occasionally also preaches at the services. She is about 43, married, has 4 children, and will be ordained in August 2020. Reverend Jennifer stated that services were switched to online only the week of March 8. In-person services have not resumed to date. Originally, the target date for the reopening was July 12. Unfortunately, there was a Covid-19 flare up in the county that week so church was not resumed.

She also explained that there were many reasons the decision was made to move to an online only format. The traditional service has many who fall into an at-risk elderly population in the congregation. In addition, the service normally has a choir and orchestra, which typically require people being close together, usually unmasked. The church also decided to follow the state government and the CEO of City Methodist Hospital recommendations by closing on Match 8. She further explained the "Methodome" United Methodist Church is the largest church in their Methodist Conference, and has the responsibility to other churches looking to it on large decisions such as shutting down in-person services. The pastors wanted to be cautious and mindful of this. In addition, the pastors have the responsibility of protecting and loving one another, with regards to community worship as well as mental health. All of these types of concerns were and will continue to be discussed when making the decision to reopen. The final decision to close was made by the board of trustees and Dr. Sam.

There were some changes Reverend Jennifer noticed in the congregation while the services have been conducted online only. At first, there were more online participants than the church ever had with in-person attendance. As time has gone on, the novelty wore off and online participation has decreased. In her perspective, people are realizing that worship really is not about entertainment. This, particularly, has been a good change and realization. The church has increased their offering of small online bible studies and participants in those have grown. Some of the participants are people from smaller churches, including some out-of-state churches who do not have the resources "Methodome" United Methodist Church has.

During the pandemic, the "Methodome "United Methodist Church started offering special prayer services online and a special racial reconciliation service. They have also offered special mission programs, like adopt-a-senior, which involves some of the congregation writing to seniors who are alone, as well as special food drives and deliveries. These have occurred and will continue until the church reopens.

When the pandemic first broke out, wedding and funeral attendance was limited to 10 persons, which was extremely difficult for families to decide who could attend. Starting in late July, attendance restrictions have been relaxed to 60 persons. Attendees are asked to sit rows apart and only in groups that they live with, such as family. There is no singing from the congregation inside allowed, but singing is allowed outside at the gravesite.

Communion was not served, since the church has been strictly online until August 2, 2020. The congregation was then offered two different options. They could have communion at their own homes with the live online service, or they could go through a drive through communion offered by the pastors at the church that evening. The pastors wore gloves and face masks while serving communion to promote a low-risk event.

The pastors stand behind the same theology regarding the pandemic and its relation to God's work in the world. They believe the pandemic is not punishment and the church is a part of a fallen world. God has allowed the pandemic to happen, since He is all-powerful and in control. At the same time, God can also bring good from it.

Congregational Response

Janice is a Caucasian woman in her early seventies, who has been a member of the "Methodome" United Methodist Church for 21 years. She is married, has 3 grandchildren, and is a retired oil and gas marketer. She agreed to being interviewed about how the pandemic has affected her church.

Janice watched most of the services online during the pandemic. She and her family wanted to stay connected to the church and connected to the Word. Her daughter set up the online sermon to connect to the TV for her to watch. She also watched her daughter's contemporary church service a few times. Janice mentioned she did not like watching the services online, as she wants to gather with other Christians. She emphasized she likes to hear the Body worship together in response and singing. Janice also noted there is comfort in having other Christians worshiping with you and feels the personal connection with others in the congregation is lost online. In saying that, she and her family will physically attend the church service as soon as the church is reopened. Her family noted this in a church survey that was sent out.

Janice felt that the transition to online only worship was fairly seamless and that the church was well-equipped, since it had previously offered online services. She made sure to note that there is not a full choir, and the few people singing were spaced out. She expressed her dismay that, at times during the live online service, they played back a previous time when the full choir was there. Since that part is not live, it gives her a feeling of going through the motions, rather than a time where the Spirit moves. She continued by saying nothing takes the place of being in the sanctuary in person.

Even though Janice feels as though the church did a good job with the technical aspects of the transition online, she does not believe the church did a satisfactory job of reaching out to her while there were no physical services. She attributes part of this to the huge size of the church. To further underscore her point, she mentioned there hasn't been any communication regarding the status of the Methodist church potential split, which is a very big deal to her, especially since one of the church pastors is on the conference committee. The annual conference had been delayed, due to the pandemic. Janice is on the church's Instagram and email distribution and still feels as if she is missing out on important church information.

Janice believes God allows all things. He could have killed the virus if He wanted to and God allowed it for good reasons such as drawing us to Him. Her view of God has not changed or been shaken by the pandemic.

Rob also agreed to be interviewed about the "Methodome" United Methodist Church during the pandemic. Rob is an 82-year-old Caucasian man who is a retired military chaplain. He is a widower, has 3 children, many grandchildren, and one great grandchild.

Rob watched the services online regularly because worship has always been in his environment and he is steadfast. He also watched other worship services within the Methodist Church because he enjoys listening to various pastors. Rob is inclined to go to church in person, but realizes it is smart to stay safe and healthy during this time of the pandemic. He prefers the physical church services, because it easier to connect with people. In addition, there is a satisfaction in worshiping with others. It is also more consistent with his routine.

Rob expressed that the "Methodome" United Methodist Church has done a pretty good job with respect to the online transition. He gets the feeling of worship even though he is not with believers. However, he did mention he would always rather prefer to be there in person and that he has not seen a high online attendance.

In Rob's view, pastors have historically shied away from addressing current issues and challenging the congregation, as they are more interested in pacifying the congregation. During the pandemic, he noticed the pastors' sermons did give more focus on challenging the congregation. He hopes this continues to awaken the spirit of the congregation. Rob stated that many members of the congregation have already given their lives to Christ, so it makes sense the sermons need to be challenging the members to grow and act deeper in their faith. Rob mentioned that pandemics can bring out the worst and best in people. He wants the pastors and congregation to focus on how they can use this time to help bring people together. He believes this is a wonderful opportunity for the church to be active and wants to see more.

Rob noted that throughout the pandemic, some more Bible studies and observances have been made available; however, he is not driven by most of those things. He would like to see more interactive things taking place. He did not mention if he was contacted as a senior, or if he had been written to or called by a member of the congregation. He did mention that he has changed his own ministry of visiting people in the hospital to calling them on the phone during this time, as he is not allowed as a hospital visitor.

Rob stated that he was not inclined to think God caused the pandemic. Rather, God is available to work through it by providing insight to those researching cures and through communities learning to help each other. Rob believes God is accessible to his people by providing guidance, wisdom, hope and strength. His view of God has not changed at all due to the pandemic.

Post Pandemic Future

With regards to the long-term effects of the pandemic, the pastors hope the strong connection between the churches in the area continues. It seems the congregation has understood, at a deeper level, the importance of community worship, and the pastors pray that this appreciation will continue to grow the congregation. Specifically, Reverend Jennifer prays the church administration realizes that pastors can be even more effective by not being in their offices from eight to five.

The pandemic has changed the way Reverend Jennifer personally sees her ministry. She now describes worship as the only thing the church really does within the building. Everything else in ministry is done outside of the church building.

Janice believes the older people in the congregation will be more cautious coming back. Janice is fairly confident that greeting others will be changed when in-person services are resumed, and is upset that she will not be able to hug others in the congregation. In addition, she thinks that since the church will potentially have less people attend when it reopens, it will be harder to love each other as the Body of Christ.

When asked about the pandemic impact on the "Methodome" United Methodist Church, Rob thought at first, it could make the church stronger and that the congregation might appreciate services more. He continued by saying there may be a heightened spirit coming back together. However, Rob thought some won't come back to church; some will slide away while others will come back stronger in their faith. With regards to the long-term future, Rob interestingly stated he didn't think there would be much impact. Historically, Rob has noticed people tend to quickly forget horrors, such as pandemics.

Reflection & the *Missio Dei*

It was a pleasure to observe and interview members of the traditional congregation of the "Methodome" United Methodist Church. As in any massive event that impacts the normal way of life, positives and negatives are revealed from the pandemic situation. A consistent message of the importance of connection was heard over and over in the sermons and interviews. From a positive aspect, the connection between churches has been made stronger due to the pandemic. On the other hand, the need for showing connection (love and support) between members of the church has been highlighted and craved during this time. This directly reflects the *Missio Dei*. God's desire is to show love and connection in a relationship with His people which God often does through others. That is why we all have this need in the first place, and why it has become prominent during the pandemic.

Though the church utilized social media for services, held special events, and created programs for the church to connect with other members in need, it still lacked the amount of emotional connection for the church body. In a sense, it was good for the church members to recognize this need, as they will probably appreciate being back together more after the pandemic. However, the church needed to look for more ways to reach out to its body as a part of the *Missio Dei*.

For example, though the adopt-a-senior program was actively happening, neither Rob nor Janice mentioned anything about it (either from the giving or recipient side). This could be due to the lack of communication of the need or the knowledge of how to go about volunteering to fill this ministry. Either way, the church could do a better job at the communication aspect in executing programs such as these. One way is to ensure that the church has relevant information on its congregation to know who is in need of connection. In addition, the volunteer process needs to be communicated well, easy to sign up for, and clearly state the volunteer job requirements. There should also be multiple ways of communicating these types of programs. It should be found on a frequently distributed newsletter via email and physical mail, as well as easily assessable on the website.

Since the majority of the congregation is elderly, it was surprising that no program was in place to help set up or troubleshoot technical type issues for these members, since they are not as familiar with social media as the rest of the population is. This would be an additional program that could be put in place or a subset of the adopt-a-senior program. Other services for the seniors could be identified through the phone calls, emails, or needs form, such as picking up groceries or helping fix things that break or need attention during the pandemic. There have been many businesses such as lawn care and maid services that have had to reduce their work, due to infected employees.

The singles demographic was not mentioned in the sermons, nor in the interviews. Since the US divorce rate is high, and knowing the "Methodome" United Methodist Church is a large church with many resources, it would be assumed there are a quite a few singles in the church population that are not necessarily elderly. Loneliness during quarantine, combined with not being able to worship with the body of believers in-person can exacerbate emotional and mental health concerns.

As part of the *Missio Dei*, it would be advantageous to the singles and the rest of the congregation to be a part of a program where singles are reached out to and loved. This could look similar to the adopt-a-senior program or singles could be targeted to serve the seniors. The latter would bring joy and interaction to the singles serving. Some single mothers could especially need some help in similar ways that the seniors could help with or financially, if they have lost their jobs through the pandemic. On the other hand, some members that have lost their jobs would have some time to volunteer to help serve other members. Obviously, there would need to be rules set in place to ensure safety measures are intact to reduce the likelihood of transferring the virus.

Another demographic that was not discussed in the interviews was the youth and children. The pandemic has also been a trying time for these teens and children, as they are accustomed to look forward to spending time with friends at camp and other summer activities. The pandemic is a wonderful opportunity to incorporate the teens and children to serve the Body of Christ. Children could make crafts or letters to give to seniors and singles. Teens can participate in more of the physical opportunities to serve other members, as well as utilizing their driver's license to deliver things! Participating in serving the rest of the church during this time will stress the importance of serving and also reinforce the theology the pastors are preaching that God can accomplish good through difficult events.

The common theme of a desire to worship with the Body of Christ was also brought up throughout the interviews. There are other ways this can be accomplished than online. In this county, there were pop-up drive-in movie theatres in Wal-Mart and Waterpark parking lots during the summer evenings. Why not do the same thing for a worship service? The services could be held in the church parking lot or high school with a large screen that projects the pastor, worship band or singer. The congregation would turn their car radios to a certain station and could even sit on or in front of their cars in lawn chairs to worship with others and still remain socially distant. Fortunately, the "Methodome" United Methodist Church has the resources available to accomplish this.

In short, the "Methodome" United Methodist Church was equipped and reacted quickly to transition the church to an online presence during the Covid-19 pandemic. They have been extremely helpful for other smaller churches to stay connected and continue to grow spiritually during this time. The pastors have done a phenomenal job of communicating how the pandemic plays into the church's theology. There were a few special programs started, to address the needs of the church during the outbreak, and more can be implemented fairly easily. The church can prepare for future events, such as this one, by exploring these program ideas, improving their communication, and clarifying information on church related events happening during a significant situation like the Covid-19 pandemic.

Case Study Six: Without Fear, We Place Our Hope in Jesus

Dylan Wilson

Dylan Wilson is the director of youth and young adult ministries at a United Methodist Church in Knoxville, Tennessee. He works to transform families, friendships, and the community through the Gospel message.

Context: Rural Indiana
Affiliation: Church of Christ
Size: 650 members

Introduction

A place. A people. A presence. Throughout the entire biblical narrative, God repeatedly returns to this one great desire: a place where God's people dwell in His presence. In the Old Testament, this was the tabernacle of the Israelite community. When Israel became an established nation, the tabernacle became a temple in Jerusalem. After Jesus' resurrection in the New Testament, the tabernacle became the human heart, and suddenly God's presence could be found where His people are, namely the church.

God's desire does not end with just a small group of people, however. God wants the entire world to be the people that dwell in His presence. Second Peter 3:9 says that God is "being patient for your sake. He does not want anyone to be destroyed, but wants everyone to repent."[1] God's desire and patience are displayed through the *Missio Dei*, or the Mission of God. From the global Church to individual local congregations, God uses His people as the primary instrument of God's mission to the ends of the earth. Included in that mission are churches

[1] All biblical references are taken from the *New Living Translation*, Tyndale House Publishers, 2015.

like "Gallaher View" Christian Church, who, in the midst of a global pandemic, are reaching their congregation with the message of God through social media platforms.

Church Context

"Gallaher View" Christian Church, a church affiliated with the Christian Church/Church of Christ movement, resides in a rural farming community in Indiana. They have five full-time pastoral staff and approximately 650 members on their roll. Prior to the coronavirus pandemic, "Gallaher View" offered three regular Sunday worship services: a traditional service at 9:00 AM; a contemporary service at 10:30 AM; and a second contemporary service at 6:00 PM in order to reach younger crowds who work shifts that do not accommodate Sunday morning worship times. This evening service was also livestreamed to Vimeo and Facebook. They provided regular youth and children's meetings, as well as adult small groups.

At the time of writing, there have been 76 confirmed COVID-19 cases[2] out of 16,350 people in the county,[3] resulting in a COVID-19 impact of just under 0.465% for the county.

Church Response & Social Media

In order to combat this pandemic, nearly every state in the U.S. recognized the importance of taking immediate preventative action around the second week of March. Schools, restaurants, and places of worship were either restricted in number or ordered to completely close, to slow the spread of the coronavirus. On Thursday, March 12, "Gallaher View" was one of these places of worship that made the difficult decision to completely close its doors to public use. However, lacking physical presence did not mean that the ministries of the church ceased. Instead, certain ministries moved online, and the church utilized platforms like Zoom, Facebook, and Vimeo in ways they had not done before. For

---

[2] "Corona Virus in the U.S.: Latest Map and Case Count" *The New York Times*. https://www.nytimes.com/interactive/2020/us/coronavirus-us-cases.html#states, accessed on August 15, 2020

[3] United States Census Bureau: Fountain County, Indiana. https://www.census.gov/quickfacts/fountaincountyindiana, accessed on August 15, 2020

example, in addition to the livestream, Sunday School classes, small groups, and youth and children's groups created Zoom classrooms in order to teach, fellowship, and pray together.

Having already had an online presence through the Sunday evening livestream, the transition to a totally online presence was technologically simple, though individual perspectives were difficult to overcome. No one on leadership wanted to close the church, but everyone knew that it was the best decision, especially considering the church's number of congregants over the age of 65. Using the projections available in March, the leadership crunched the numbers and determined that at least three people in the congregation would die from the disease. When put in this eye-opening context, the decision became much easier to make, though some changes to the online format needed to be made.

Pastor James, the senior minister at "Gallaher View" for more than 20 years, said, "Previously, we were recording the night contemporary service and putting that online. This was our effort to reach the younger crowd who were working swing shifts. However, we recognized that that service would not work quite as well in reaching all of our congregants. So, our streamed service is now a blended service, though it follows the same basic format."

This format includes pre- and post-service Bible reading, music that revolves around the theme of the sermon, and a communion meditation that includes instructions for receiving the elements at home. During the four-week period beginning with April 12 and ending on May 3, various church leaders utilized scripture and sermon exposition to reference how God might lead the church through this pandemic. In his April 12 message, Pastor James proposed that the resurrection of Jesus Christ gives the church hope in this life, yet also reminds God's people that the best is yet to come. "The resurrection texts should inspire us to place our hope in Jesus and not live in fear about our situation," he said. "We've been reminded by COVID that this world will never completely satisfy us. It will never be the paradise that we hope for."

April 19 marked the beginning of a new sermon series through the Gospel of John. This transition meant that relating God's Word to the coronavirus pandemic would come indirectly, and only as conveniently as each week's text would allow. For example, the April 19 pre-service text, John 1, allowed the worship pastor to reflect on how this text can encourage the church during times of social distancing. "Even though we have to practice social distancing," he said, "Jesus didn't distance himself from us, but he came to us in the Word."

The following week, April 26, Pastor James addressed the pandemic in a different way. Though there was no direct relation of the scripture text (John 2:1-11) to the pandemic, as with the previous week, Pastor James disclosed his own struggles during the service: "I thought I was doing well with missing everyone, but even phone calls make it difficult. I desire so much for the church to return to in-person worship as safely and as quickly as possible." Later in the service, as the focus turned toward communion, the meditation reminded listeners that the church throughout history has had to meet in strange places. Yet, regardless of the forces surrounding them, they continued to gather around the Lord's table.

The May 3 service contained both direct scripture references as well as pastoral exposition on the coronavirus pandemic. At the beginning of the service, two young people were baptized. "God's kingdom is moving on in spite of all the things that we are facing," observed the worship pastor. Later in the service, during the message on discipleship (John 3), a reference to Numbers 21 reminded the church that God has repeatedly delivered his people from all sorts of dangers— and this virus is no different. This service ended with an announcement that the elders and staff were to have a meeting that afternoon to determine a plan to reopen the church building— a meeting that saw the board approve an outdoor drive-in service and, eventually, a limited-capacity indoor service.

Pastoral Approach

Sunday services are only a fraction of what a church typically does to engage its people in ministry. There are many planned and unplanned gatherings throughout the week that arguably make up a large portion of a church's ministry effort. While a great deal of effort was aimed at refining the use of online platforms, and as important as the internet is to daily life in 2020, it is not the only form of communication available during times of social distancing. Pastor James personally prefers communicating with others face-to-face, and the next best thing for him is a simple phone call.

"As best we could, we tried to use the phone to connect with people," he said. "I would make about twenty-five phone calls every day, just to touch base with people and see how they were doing. We were also aware of when people would be in the hospital or had other similar needs. While we were not permitted to visit these facilities, we would call and pray with them over the phone."

This effort was made easier due to the congregation's structure. "Gallaher View"'s goal is to have every single congregation member participate in "Shepherd Groups." These groups are led by individuals that seek to minister to and connect with each member individually and collectively. While the effectiveness of each group varies, it is this structure that allowed Pastor James to reach out by phone to each member. He was about 80% effective at establishing contact with this method, and many people were glad to hear from him.

The congregation also faced regular life events, such as weddings and funerals. Funerals were particularly complicated by social distancing mandates. Visitation times were shortened considerably. Masks were required during the entire service, though Pastor James would take his off during his speaking portions. Many families were more cautious than Pastor James regarding physical contact. For example, several people preferred elbow bumps over shaking hands.

"During this time, it is difficult to determine what is going to be the most effective way to show love and support to people that are either hurting or are starting new chapters in their lives," Pastor James said. "The funeral directors in this area tend to be especially cognizant of the spiritual needs of the families. For example, although the government wants gatherings to be restricted to ten people, funeral homes were not going to run people off. They allowed families and ministers to do what they felt was right for the family."

Pastoral care is not the only responsibility of the minister. Pastors are also expected to interpret world events through a theological lens.

For Pastor James, he sees two ways that the pandemic is related to God's work in our world.

"I believe that this is something that God has allowed to happen to draw humankind's attention to our lack of control and our own vulnerability," he said. "We don't have control over a lot of things like we think we do. There is also an opportunity for 'fence-riders' (people uncertain about God's role in their personal lives) to pay more attention to what's going on in their lives. We've seen people who are mad at God, but we've also seen people who are responding appropriately."

Church Response

Others in the congregation interpreted the pandemic differently. Andrew is a young adult who came through the church's youth ministry and has been a participant in the church's functions for about fifteen years. He believes that God has not really been involved in the pandemic at all. Instead, he wonders why Christians need to interpret everything theologically.

"This pandemic wasn't a surprise to God," Andrew said. "Why should we spiritualize something that doesn't need to be spiritualized? The pandemic has been driven by humankind's actions, not divine causation."

Gracie, another young adult who started at the church in the children's ministry and has been a regular attender for twenty years, agreed. "I don't think God caused the pandemic," she said. "Working at a health clinic gives me firsthand experience that this virus is a real thing. But I don't think God caused it."

If God did not cause the pandemic, one might wonder what *did* cause it. Marcus has been attending the church for thirteen years, and is currently in his final year of a five-year term as an elder. He has been a school teacher for more than twenty years and an assistant principal for the last two. He suggests that sin is the central problem.

"It all goes back to Eden," Marcus explained. "Humans were never designed to be sick. We were designed to be joyful and connected to God.

When sin entered the world, so did sickness and death— that includes this pandemic. It has been about 100 years since the last pandemic, so everyone is experiencing this for the first time. But this is not new to the world or God."

In spite of wrestling with the theological difficulties a pandemic raises, Pastor James, Andrew, Gracie, and Marcus all agreed that God is in control and that everything will turn out according to God's purposes and plan.

"If God wanted to put an end to all of this, he could simply speak that into existence," reflected Marcus. "My faith hasn't been shaken. Instead, I think there are valuable lessons to be learned all around."

"God is good, and I've seen his goodness evidenced by the fact that I work in the medical field, yet I haven't caught the virus," Gracie said. "I do my best to practice the wisdom and counsel told to us by experts, and I am sure that God plays a part in honoring our efforts to make wise decisions."

While the church staff navigated the difficulties of the effects of the pandemic on their respective ministries, they were not the only ones who were impacted by the social distancing mandates. Marcus' experience as a school teacher provided him with a unique perspective on these effects. He claims that schools attempt to balance mental health and physical health, while churches attempt to balance both of these with an added focus on spiritual health. In his assessment, the greatest area impacted by the pandemic has been communal life.

"If there's a place for people to find meaning, purpose, and fulfillment, it's at church," he said. "You can do that online, but you're missing the physical face-to-face encounter. There are people that are begging for physical connection, but that just has to wait right now."

Andrew and Gracie also emphasized the need for face-to-face interaction. "The absence of physical church services has mainly affected me socially," Andrew said. "The lacking fellowship makes an impact. My spiritual life doesn't cease to exist, but interpersonal relationships and small groups are far more important to me."

"Without the presence, you don't get the full effect of the church," Gracie said. "It's not about the building, it's about the people. Conversing with someone in-person is different than commenting on a Facebook thread and simply saying 'hi.'"

Marcus concurs. "There have been fewer personal connections lately," he said. "The ability to connect with and check in with people is not as convenient. Accountability, mental health, and other similar personal areas are all affected by this pandemic. However, I think the social aspect is missed the most."

Pastor James noticed that church congregants seemed to experience a significant disconnect due to the uncertainty about what they could or could not do. He views the online service as better than nothing— but just barely.

Andrew agreed. "I did not watch the church's online services each week," he said. "I don't like online. It felt very impersonal when it came to worship. The sermons were good overall, but I'm also easily distracted."

In addition to the social aspects, Pastor James also noticed differences in the attitudes of people, especially where restrictions on youth and children's ministries are concerned.

"The biggest change was the attitudes of people," Pastor James explained. "From conversations I've had with people, once youth and children's ministry functions resume, we expect to see a great increase in the amount of people that return. People have literally told me, 'As soon as the kid stuff starts, we're back.'"

Post-Pandemic Future

Following the aforementioned May 3 leadership meeting, the church has indeed resumed in-person gatherings through the drive-in service and a limited-capacity indoor service. The drive-in service has especially given people, who, from Pastor James' perspective, are getting tired of the pandemic and being told what to do, an opportunity to exercise some control in their lives. However, church leaders are exercising caution about resuming other regular ministry functions, such as youth and children's activities. Although this leads to less in-person attendance, church leadership compassionately understands that some families would prefer to stay home so they can keep their children content.

Many churches are eagerly waiting for their in-person attendance to return to or even surpass their pre-pandemic numbers. At "Gallaher View," some people Pastor James expected to be there immediately have not shown up yet, and others he did not expect to be there have not missed a gathering. Pastor James offered his thoughts: "At this point, it's not a true picture of what the church will be like. I think our numbers will increase because there have been several families that have indicated that they want to join the church. However, I think it will be July 2021 before we return to where we were before this pandemic began."

In some ways, the pandemic has also had a positive effect on the church. Gracie and Marcus both sense that people are slowing down and paying closer attention to their families and to God.

"I think people are spending more time with their families and less time on their phones," Gracie said. "They're actually paying attention to the people in their lives. God might be using this pandemic to help us focus on the things that really matter."

Marcus agreed. "Under normal circumstances, it is easier to ignore God," he explained. "When you're attending to the daily needs of life, it is very easy for God to take the backseat. When life slows down, you get the chance to appreciate the minor things and spend time in prayer, in reading [the Bible], and with God. He may not be actively grabbing our attention, but the opportunity is suddenly more apparent. If you're looking for God, he's right there."

The effects of the pandemic are not only for the short-term, however. There are certainly going to be long-term effects in multiple areas, including attendance, ministry structures, and the role online church will play once restrictions are lifted. Pastor James shared his thoughts on how the pandemic might change the way church is done in the future— both throughout the global church and at "Gallaher View."

"Most congregations that have added an online service will and should continue those services, although those services are going to be a drain on the in-person services," he said. "We will absolutely continue our online service long after this pandemic is over. It is vital to have it these days. However, I think people will eventually figure out that online services simply do not provide what being in person does provide. The scripture says, 'Do not forsake gathering together.'[4] Online services do not provide the fullness of encouragement needed to sustain the church. It is the participation *in* the actions of the church, like worship, the sermon, and communion, not just *receiving* those things, that offer the most encouragement."

Although the online service cannot meet all of the needs of the church, Pastor James does believe that the current generation of tech-savvy individuals are going to turn away from churches that do not provide *something* online. Without an online platform, churches inadvertently communicate to this group of people that there is no place for them. He sees a correlation between the online church platform and the way Americans do their online shopping.

"An online presence is a great way for seekers to test the waters before they actually visit your church," he explained. "The greatest component is the in-person service, but the online platform is a fantastic stepping stone. When we shop online, we can usually get a free sample before we actually purchase the item we want. That's the mentality in America right now, and that is certainly an aspect of online church."

Gracie agrees with Pastor James' assessment. "Positively, there can be great outreach through the livestream," she said. "However, recent building projects may not be utilized according to their intended purpose due to the ease of the livestream. While I personally would prefer to go to church, the livestream is just easier."

Andrew also believes that the online platform is geared for seekers far more than established Christians, but he thinks the long-term effects will be much more drastic. He predicts many rapid changes, such as fewer people entering full time vocational ministry, adoption of an "anytime, anywhere" church model, and more small groups and

[4] Hebrews 10:25.

in-home ministries. Churches will continue with their specialized ministries, like youth groups, but parents and families will become equipped to operate at home. In his view, it will be critically important for churches to designate responsibility by acquiring mature Christians that can authentically connect with and shepherd other Christians.

"The 'one-size-fits-all' church model isn't going to last much longer," he said. "This is a time for us to start re-evaluating, 'Is what we're doing working, and is it going to continue to work?'"

Marcus agrees that there will be changes. For him, these changes are primarily in terms of momentum and the online platform's ability to emphasize personal sensitivities and preferences. Marcus sees momentum as being measured in numbers, but it is also measured in the people who receive help financially, mentally, and emotionally. It is measured in the people who are growing spiritually, who are getting their lives on track, and who are taking steps toward becoming who they want to be. Measuring these aspects has been difficult during this time since people are limited in how much contact they can have with one another. However, while the pandemic has disrupted everyone's momentum, it has also opened more opportunities to be sensitive to what others are comfortable with, like shaking hands.

"This experience will allow us to be more mindful of other situations going forward," Marcus explained. "There's a portion of the population that are overwhelmed with a large crowd and being too close to other people. There are always going to be people that don't want to skip church, but for some special situations— like the elderly, flu season, and even slick roads— it might not be safe to leave the house. The online platform allows for them to participate in spite of circumstances that might prohibit physical gatherings. Not everyone is as comfortable as I am. Now we can understand each other and approach one another with more respect and sensitivity."

Reflection & *Missio Dei*

Respect and sensitivity capture two core elements of the *Missio Dei*. When dealing with people, especially during times of uncertainty and potential global crisis, respect and sensitivity mark the difference between an effective ministry and one that is disregarded as irrelevant. For example, missionaries throughout church history have experienced success or failure based on respect or lack of respect for the culture they were trying to reach. The Jesuits were especially mindful of respect and sensitivity. Francis Xavier (1506-1552) learned many local languages as he spread the Gospel to India, Japan, and Borneo. Matteo Ricci (1552-1610) spread the Gospel in China by adopting Chinese dress, referring to Confucian teachings and rules of life, and introducing scientific discoveries. It is necessary for the church to pay close attention to the movements of the culture and respond accordingly.

Likewise, it appears that "Gallaher View" is practicing respect and sensitivity in their culture as they navigate reopening the church and reintroducing ministries to their congregation. In an area with such a marginal COVID impact, the church can proceed by cautiously resuming ministry functions while also offering grace to those who may choose to refrain from participating. While the spirit of many is to be more than willing to participate when an opportunity arises, there are also many who are waiting to return. If someone is new to the church, one of the first questions asked concerns what the newcomers are comfortable with regarding physical contact. This type of respect and sensitivity will surely prove effective throughout the life of the church as they seek to continue their participation in the *Missio Dei*.

In spite of the pandemic-related obstacles facing "Gallaher View," the church has found alternative ways to carry out the *Missio Dei*. As previously noted, the online worship services and phone calls are currently the standard methods of sharing God's message with people. These methods are also laced with opportunities to pray for and with congregants and other members of the community. While these are the primary modes of operation, there are two others apparent in "Gallaher View"'s current praxis: preservation of life and youth service.

Perhaps an overlooked aspect of the *Missio Dei* is the respect for and preservation of life, as demonstrated in "Gallaher View"'s careful approach to in-person worship. The figures provided in the latest COVID reports might seem like arbitrary numbers. However, doing the math, as "Gallaher View"'s leadership did, allows one to understand the gravity of the situation of the world. They were able to determine that, according to trends, at least three congregants— mothers, fathers, friends— could die from this disease. For "Gallaher View," "three" is three, and three are too many. God values each of these people in their community, and in order to faithfully participate in the *Missio Dei*, the church needed to take the pandemic seriously so as to safeguard even these three.

The church was also able to resume limited youth activities. During the last week of July, the youth group was permitted to take a week-long, out-of-state trip to serve with Habitat for Humanity. They were able to tangibly bring God's presence to people who needed help. In doing so, they extended the *Missio Dei* even beyond their own state's borders, especially at a time where uncertainty, anxiety, and worry are immensely prevalent.

For all of the good things "Gallaher View" is doing to be a good presence in their community, there are three areas that are worth critically evaluating in search of refinement. The first is the online presence. While the church is clearly present online, some congregants found it difficult to give their full attention to the weekly service. This was partially due to the length of the services.[5] For "Gallaher View," leadership may ask, "Is the current length of our service a help or a hindrance in reaching our community?" Indeed, all churches with an online presence ought to ask this question regularly.

The second area worth critically evaluating is the church's current online ministry to children. The sentiment from Pastor James is that the online service is not reaching everyone, especially younger kids. This reality is emphasized by Pastor James' observation that the church's reopening attendance could be as much as 25% higher if youth and children's functions were available. Until these ministries resume, leadership may ask, "What could we do to intentionally reach the children in our community?"

The third area worth critically evaluating is the church's desire and subsequent ability to reach young adults. This is not an area that is isolated to just "Gallaher View." In a 2019 Barna Group study, just over half (54%) of 18-to-35-year-old Christians attend church at least

[5] The average length for the 4 services between April 12 and May 3 was over 1 hour.

once a month. The sentiment among Andrew and Gracie, both young adults at "Gallaher View" and regular attenders, is that there is room for improvement. Involvement in small groups is the primary emphasis for growth, but even these groups are not specialized specifically for young adults. As Gracie observed, "There has been a gap in ministering to young adults for some time, but that gap is even bigger right now." Reflecting on young adult ministry, leadership may ask, "How can the church close the gap in ministering to young adults?"

In terms of the leadership's heart and willingness, the church has done well. They have attempted to help as many people grow as much as they can. They are anxiously waiting to fully reopen the church and engage in the totality of their ministries again. Finally, they are excited for the day that they get to have a greater impact on the community.

Going forward, "Gallaher View"'s participation in the *Missio Dei* will likely continue to change. Even when the pandemic fades, church functions will never be the same. While they have no intention to cease their worship livestream, no comment was made about the continuation of other online ministries, like youth group or other small groups. It could be to the church's benefit to maintain some sort of online presence in these areas, especially as church culture increasingly adopts an "anytime, anywhere" model. While the community is not a leading-edge community in terms of new ministry developments, the church should also not be surprised to find family groups seeking resources in order to engage in the mission of the church from home. Finally, though it is currently restricted, the church will always have a physical presence. The importance of face-to-face communication can never be overemphasized, though the pandemic has brought into sharp focus just how important physical contact is to a whole community. Time, effort, and resources should be spent toward various platforms in appropriate measure, but "Gallaher View"'s best effort in the *Missio Dei* will depend on their sustainable physical presence for years to come.

Ethnographic Reports from December 2020

Case Study Seven: Hope is Still Found in Jesus

Sarah Walker

Sarah Walker is a current MDiv student at Asbury Theological Seminary that claims Knoxville, TN as her home. When she's not studying, you can find her playing with her dog, Luna, traveling (pre-pandemic), and trying new restaurants.

Context: Rural Tennessee
Affiliation: Wesleyan-based
Size: About 200 in attendance

Introduction

There are many times in the Bible where God reminds us to slow down and breathe. Even after creating the heavens and the Earth, God himself rested. Now, in 2019/2020, He is forcing a world focused on having everything immediately and faster than ever, to take a step back and remember what his purpose is. For a small rural church in Tennessee, slowing down and showing God's love is easy in normal circumstances, but when a global pandemic is taken into effect, it had to find ways to rise to the occasion and continue on its mission.

The novel Coronavirus, COVID-19, "The Rona," – whatever it may be referred to as, the pandemic that began in late fall/ early winter of 2019, has taken the world by storm and affected more people than ever anticipated. What started out as a faraway disease has now slowly taken over the world and shaped the way the United States of America and other countries function daily. Churches are not immune to the changing climate and have been affected just as hard, if not worse, by COVID-19. All around the country, churches were scrambling to find a way to still reach the community, but also keep as many people in their congregations as safe as possible, as the entire world shut down.

For larger congregations in bigger cities, this may not have felt like a huge issue. It may have been weird to transition to an online-only platform, but many larger churches already recorded their weekly sermons. In many cases, there was only a small pivot that was made – sermons recorded in a more intimate setting, worship in a smaller studio versus on a large stage, announcements filmed and sent out. Perhaps there was already an online platform in place for the members of their church – where information could easily be sent out and accessed. With a large budget and technological teams already in place, the more daunting question of whether or not quarantine will last until Easter was in the forefront of their minds. Many of the skills, equipment and resources were already in place. Smaller churches did not have the same luxury.

Church Context

Nestled in the rural part of northern middle Tennessee near the Kentucky border, is a Wesleyan-based First Church of God. Known for its proximity to the creek, "Good Lord Willin' and the Creek Don't Rise" can be found printed on the bulletin every Sunday. At this church, most of the congregation is related in one way or another. Even the pastor considers the majority of the members his kin and is fondly referred to as "Brother Geoff." Members of the church may attend for years before knowing what "Bubba," the associate pastor's real name is. Those who are not related by blood are considered family and welcomed with open arms to all the family functions.

There is a slower way of life overall in their town, and most Sunday mornings are like coming home to a family reunion. With a combination of traditional hymns and more contemporary songs during worship, the Church at the Creek does a really good job of reaching both their older and younger generations. There is even a "special music" portion of the Sunday morning service, where a member of the congregation may sing or one of the many children programs throughout the year will perform their final show. The Church at the Creek personifies the body of Christ and knows what it means to love like Jesus.

When the pandemic was only an epidemic, it seemed very far away from Tennessee. As it loomed closer and closer, larger cities like Memphis, Nashville, and Knoxville seemed to feel the effects a lot sooner, and on a larger scale, than the smaller rural areas. It was for this reason the Church at the Creek may not have been as prepared for the gigantic shift from a typical in person Sunday service to only having online resources as larger churches were. Before diving into the challenges this church faced, it is important to understand the outside factors that also affected their ability to respond and other valuable resources that they already had in place.

Call it serendipity and the divine hand of God, but there were many decisions previously implemented that, in turn, helped with the response to COVID-19. As previously mentioned, the town the Church at the Creek is located in is very rural. For many years, satellite tv and internet were the only available options. Many residents have a home phone because of the lack of service and accessible internet. A few months prior to the pandemic, one of the larger power companies came together with other companies and members of the community to finally roll out the new cable and internet initiative that brought high-speed fiber into the homes of everyone in the county. At the end of 2019, the church had made the decision to triple the budget used for assisting congregation members and people in the community that are in need. Finally, since the 1990s, the pastor of the church has emailed out a text of the Sunday morning message to anyone subscribed to the email messages and posted it to the church's Facebook page as well.

Church Response & Social Media

On March 15, 2020, the Church at the Creek had its last in person service for a while. The decision to suspend in person gatherings and quarantine in the state of Tennessee influenced their decision to close the doors as well. At this time, the area where the church is located had not received the new fiber internet connection. This led the pastor, Brother Geoff, to get creative with his messages and how to communicate them. He effectively filmed videos in locations relative to his message and then uploaded the videos to the church's Facebook page. A link to the video was also included in the weekly email that was distributed. In order to allow the congregation to worship each week, YouTube videos of songs with lyrics were shared via the Facebook page. A video recording of the pastor playing and singing "Sanctuary," the way the service is typically closed every week, was also repeatedly shared in order to have the continuity that would be found at an in-person meeting.

Easter Sunday came with the reminder of God's promise – He has risen indeed. The Facebook video of the week featured Brother Geoff walking down a road near his home. As he walked, he read Luke 24:13-15 and acted out the walking the two apostles did in the scripture. From there, he began his sermon with a glimpse of hope – "First, I'm reminded that no event in history has shaped the world like the life, death, and resurrection of Jesus Christ. And second, I'm reminded of this simple fact about life: It doesn't go on forever. There is death, and every one of us must face our mortality."

Even in the midst of a pandemic and any other turmoil the world and nation was facing, Brother Geoff reminded his congregation that hope can be found in Jesus and the fact that He is alive. He took a yearly message on the resurrection and incorporated the real and raw events that his members were facing. Worship was in the form of three songs: *Because He Lives* by Bill & Gloria Gaither, *The Easter Song* by Keith Green, and *Sanctuary* – recorded, played, and sung by the pastor himself. The lyrics "And because He lives, I can face tomorrow. Because He lives, all fear is gone. Because I know He holds the future and life is worth a living just because He lives,"[1] drove his message home.

The week after Easter, April 19, 2020, marked a month since the Church at the Creek last had an in-person service. Brother Geoff read from Act 7:55-60 and recorded his video this time from the basketball court in the church's Life Enhancement Center. He then mentioned how much he missed seeing everyone in person and that, while technology is a great tool, it was not the same. By illustrating a story both literally and figuratively about a three-year-old shooting a basketball with all the assistance from his uncle and cheering out "all by myself,"[2] and tying it to Stephen questioning the religious leaders, the pastor set the stage for

---

[1] Bill and Gloria Gaither. "Because He Lives" Hope Publishing, 1971. Public Domain.

[2] Max Lucado. *Outlive Your Life: You Were Made to Make a Difference* (Nashville: Thomas Nelson, 2010).

the main focus of the message. Even as he was dying, Stephen asked the Lord not to hold the sins against the people who were sinning against him.[3] Brother Geoff goes on to explain that one of those people was Saul, who later became the apostle Paul. He described how humans cannot do it on their own and must rely on God, but that at the end of the day, what seems like the end of a battle (i.e. Stephen being stoned to death) could be just the beginning (i.e. Paul's faithfulness and contribution to the church).

All of this, went back to reference how the church interacts with people around it, especially those who do not follow God. Most specifically, in a time of a pandemic, opting to bash medical professionals on social media and claim that a mask is unnecessary and will not be worn under any conditions – even in the event that it has been proven to prevent the spread of the disease did not show God's love. Finally, he ended with; "Tough times are here. Our faith will be tested indirectly if not directly. Some of what's happening will make it look as though we've lost this battle; but with Christ, we will eventually win the war. Yes, dastardly things may wreak havoc on us; *dastardly things may* even *demolish our body, but our soul is held safe within the arms of God.* Don't forget; just remember: *You just remember who holds you!*"

The songs for worship that followed the message included You Can Have Me by Sidewalk Prophets (YouTube song with lyrics), the hymn *Take My Life and Let It Be* (YouTube song with lyrics), and the recording of *Sanctuary*. All three of these songs were a good reminder to the body of the church that its members are supposed to give themselves to the Lord for His use. Part of the Sidewalk Prophets song was even referenced during the sermon for this exact reason: "If I saw You on the street, / and You said come and follow Me, / but I had to give up everything— / all I once held dear and all of my dreams. / Would I love You enough to let go,/ or would my love run dry / when You asked for my life? When did love become unmoving? / When did love become unconsuming? / Forgetting what the world has told me, / Father of love, you can have me!"[4]

---

[3] Acts 7:60.

[4] Sidewalk Prophets. "You Can Have Me" Word Records, 2010.

When April 26, 2020 arrived, Brother Geoff started his weekly video off by explaining the church was continuing to try and gage the future, just as everyone else is in the uncertain times. He mentioned that the church was working on a way to transition back to regular services, but that it would look different for a while and to keep the faith that God had it. In this video, the pastor is sitting outside by a wood pile on his farm. While the video from the middle of April only briefly included discussing the pandemic directly, it did have an overarching theme that was applicable to the time and was in reference to Acts 8:14-24. The woodpile helped give vision to the story he told about the owner of a firewood factory that replaced his workers with a machine when they were no longer rendering good employment. When he realized how much more wood was being cut and that the power behind the machine is what allowed it to happen, he was amazed.

Brother Geoff referenced The Newsboys song, *Way Beyond Myself*, and explained the change of heart and change of life in a particular way: "I've been thinking it's about time / to win the war that fights against all the lies invading my mind. / You have brought me to my senses: /even though You built this world to shake, / You still love me in a personal way. / So I think it's time to leave my doubt behind. / There's so much more than meets the eye / or what's going on inside. / I believe in something way beyond myself. / *Like the wind that moves the leaves, / Lord, you move me to my knees. I believe in something way beyond myself.*"[5] The message focused on the continuation of seeking out the Holy Spirit every day, not only when the relationship with God is new. In doing so, God will provide His power in all things big and small. Although it did not directly correlate with the pandemic, the message was one that members could apply to the current hardships they were facing by choosing God and the Holy Spirit every day, even in uncertainty.

By May 3, 2020, Brother Geoff was still posting videos that matched the theme of his message, but had stopped mentioning the pandemic as a focal point in the video. The new normal of the Sunday morning message had become Facebook videos with an active location relevant to the message. In this particular video, the pastor had recorded himself outside his barn and incorporated a large bell that was already on his land. This tied in with a story about the Liberty Bell and a continuous

[5] The Newsboys. "Way Beyond Myself" InPop Records, 2010.

metaphor about the crack in it. Brother Geoff wanted to instill to the members of his church that everyone is essential to the Kingdom of God.

The scripture reading was from Acts 8:26-35 and painted a picture that even those who seem the most unlikely to join the Kingdom are still welcome and offered grace. By using the music *Tell Them* by Andrae Crouch & The Disciples (YouTube), *Rediscover You* by Starfield (YouTube with lyrics), and *Sanctuary*, Brother Geoff tied together all aspects of his sermon. He even uses Rediscover You by Starfield to "explain their yearning to get back their passion for evangelism—to recapture their desire to spread the love and grace and mercy of God to whatever part of the world they can reach: 'You told me, / look for You and I will find. / So I'm here / like I'm searching for the first time. / Revive me, Jesus. / Make this cold heart start to move. / Help me rediscover You.'"[6]

In the time since May 3, 2020, the Church at the Creek has continued to develop its online presence. At first, the church set up a local radio station that allowed its members to drive to the parking lot at church and listen to the message while being within proximity to the church building and each other. After the fiber internet was installed, the possibilities of live streaming the service across different platforms including Facebook and YouTube became possible.

In the beginning, Brother Geoff spoke on Sunday mornings outside the front door of the church, but was eventually able to transition back into the sanctuary as businesses started opening up again in Tennessee. With most of the congregation finally having reliable internet, most Sunday School classes, the youth group, and other small groups could meet online via Zoom. In person meetings for these small groups have not fully returned as Sunday services did, but in some cases that is okay. The Church at the Creek supports a family in Mexico that can now join Bible study over Zoom and allow members of the family and the congregation to interact when no one has had the opportunity to meet in person prior to this time. Corey, the main person who is connected with the church, considers himself a member of the congregation and is excited to finally interact and meet with people in his church family.

---

[6] Starfield. "Rediscover You" Capitol CMG, 2010.

However, as mentioned previously, it took a while for the full effects of COVID-19 to hit the rural area the Church at the Creek is located in. Come November 2020, the virus spread through the congregation and even the pastor had it. During this time, the church did not meet in person for three more Sundays while Brother Geoff picked back up by creating videos around his farm and posting them on the Facebook page. What he finds interesting is, the videos that receive the most engagement on the Facebook page are the ones that are not of him in the pulpit, but the videos where he is on his farm, in his home, or in a location that is relevant to the message. Having the mentality only a prior journalist would have, Brother Geoff believes the frame of the more "relaxed" videos may be enough to make someone stop scrolling long enough to watch it. It creates an environment that feels more welcome, like talking to a friend and grabs someone's attention long enough to make them curious. The video from Easter Sunday alone had over 2,600 views!

Pastoral Approach

Brother Geoff has seen an increase in engagement with his congregation since making the change to going online. There are still people who will come in person, others who prefer to be present by sitting in their cars in the parking lot, and finally those who opt to stay home to watch. He knows of members who have not stepped foot in the church building in over a year, but are now watching the videos each week, are the ones commenting the most, and are sparking a conversation that may have never happened. The pastor believes that the pandemic has forced a lot of people out of the church building and to realize what the Bible defines as "church." It has also forced the church body to step up and embrace the changing technology. Brother Geoff said, "When we are forced into change, it becomes the new transitional stage. As long as we are alive, we are in transition.

Large gatherings are the first thing Brother Geoff believes to be changed. Many people put off memorial services for loved ones who passed away, but now, is it too late to have one when larger groups of people are allowed again? Weddings have become more intimate, with maybe 10 people in attendance, instead of 150+. The weddings, or at least the receptions, may go back to the way they were before, but the memorial services may really become a large group gathering at the grave site. The memorial services from when the pandemic first began, and even up until recently, may still be something that does not happen.

Technology is all about how you use it and view it. We have to ask ourselves, are we going to embrace it and work with it, or get left behind?"[7] He believes that many of the technological updates the church has made will be around for a while, even after the pandemic is gone.

Not all of the members of the community are embracing the technological changes. First, there are members coming to the pastor who are worried about the numbers dropping in person from almost 200 every week to less than 50. What they are missing is the engagement Brother Geoff mentioned and how many people the videos are actually reaching. Then, you have members of the congregation like Luke, who, prior to the pandemic led one of the Sunday School classes. Although other classes have used Zoom, he refuses to, stating that it interferes too much with communication. While he agrees with the decision to go online and, since his personal internet has been upgraded to fiber, prefers to watch the Sunday morning service live in his home, Zoom is one technology he cannot get behind. However, he does not see a better way for the church to meet in those groups right now, other than by using Zoom.

Other elderly members of the church initially started out by continuing to meet in person. The associate pastor, Bubba, spearheaded the communication and organization of their small group. Due to the fact many of them do not have a large online presence, if any, Bubba would call to give them updates and touch base. Many of the older adults in their bible study would not come to a Sunday morning service. However, they came on Saturday nights since the majority of their class was in the same age group, were taking similar precautions, and were always the same people who were there each week. This allowed them to still get the fellowship and word each week, without having to compromise their health or struggle to use technology they may not even have.

If the church does not embrace the technological changes, though, it will get left in the dark. Brother Geoff mentioned how, when

---

7 Brother Geoff, personal interview, December 1, 2020

the radio came out, the church freaked out and saw it as a horrible thing. When television came out, the same thing happened. What the world is facing now is a permanent change in the way technology is used and how businesses and the church can use it to stay relevant, up to date, and reach even more people.[8]

Congregational Response

Luke was also a council member at the time the Church at the Creek was discussing reopening and having in person services again. He was able to lend some insight into the questions that were being asked and how thoroughly the council had to work to make a plan.

First, there was the decision on where to host the service. The Life Enhancement Center offered an option with more room to spread out, individual hard plastic chairs, tile floors, higher ceilings and more doors to air the area out. While the sanctuary had pews that were closer together, upholstery that is harder to clean, and was more of an enclosed space, the Life Enhancement Center severely limited the technology and broadcasting capabilities between the online platforms and the radio station. Therefore, the church opted to hold service in the sanctuary, but set up an "overflow" area in the basement, where a tv was set up with the live stream of the service and members had more options to distance themselves from others.

Another great point was brought up by Luke. Right now, churches are facing a problem of trying to balance the spiritual needs with the worldly physical requirements during a pandemic. He even mentions, "the temptation is always to say 'God will provide, God will protect, and go.' But God helps those who help themselves. He never said 'tempt me and try me.' He never said 'jump off a cliff and see if I'll catch you' which is different from slipping off a cliff."[9] Both Luke and Brother Geoff mentioned that the beginning of the pandemic brought a decrease in the number of people asking the church for assistance. On an individual level, people like Luke, and other council members, were called on to assist in situations where people needed help and the church was not sure who else to call. This helped him to feel as though he were still

[8] Brother Geoff, personal interview, December 1, 2020.

[9] Luke, personal interview, November 27, 2020.

providing service and were able to minister to people, even though the doors to the physical church building were not open.

Next, the counsel had to decide if there were going to be greeters at the door on Sunday. Typically, the greeter would offer a handshake or hug and pass out the bulletins for the week. Ultimately, it was decided to put the bulletins on the entry table with hand sanitizer nearby to decrease the touching and spreading of germs, but to keep the greeter at the door to limit the amount of contact made with the door knob. Now, instead of a hug or a handshake, a nice wave and good morning has to suffice. Finally, the council decided to replace all of the air filters on the air handling system to the best ones available, to filter out as much as possible. In the end, these precautions allowed the members of the church to finally return. Although, not everyone was happy or comfortable.

Ginger, who is the secretary on the council, ran into some issues of her own. She, like Luke, prefers to watch the Sunday morning services in her home. As a high-risk member of the church, she takes the pandemic seriously since the church originally closed. Being in rural Tennessee and not seeing a spike in cases led many church members and council members to disregard the mask mandate or social distance. This put her in a situation where she felt uncomfortable and had to move to a different seat during meetings to properly social distance herself. In those instances, she brought her mask, Clorox wipes, and hand sanitizer.

While there was the option to join in via Zoom, as the secretary it was harder to keep up with the meeting and ended up not working as well as the council had hoped. There were other instances where members of the church came to a Sunday service while awaiting a COVID-19 test result, only to find out by Monday or Tuesday that they were positive. This makes Ginger wary that things may never go back to normal. Not because she does not trust God, but because she does not trust other people and cannot risk her own health.[10]

Ultimately, the biggest struggle Brother Geoff has faced since returning to in person services is the political persuasion around the virus and the effect it has on people. He recalls a conversation he had with

[10] Ginger, personal interview, November 28, 2020.

a member of his church where they mentioned "if Walmart requires me to wear a mask then I'm not going back to Walmart," with the inference that the same was true about the church.[11] Instead of having that mindset, Brother Geoff is hoping that a spiritual blessing of the pandemic will be the church shedding the attitude of "if you want to be a Christian, then come to church and we'll show you how" and instead that the church will be the hands and feet outside of the physical building. As far as the future of the church, Brother Geoff, Luke, and Ginger all agree that most, if not all, of the technological advances made by the church are here to stay. The biggest difference may be the way Sunday School and other gatherings are treated and handled once the pandemic is over.

God does not call the equipped, He equips the called. Just like he did with Moses in the Bible, He does the same with the members of His church. Brother Geoff of the Church at the Creek likes to say he was a writer that God called to be a preacher.[12] The current pandemic has called everyone in the world to reevaluate their lives. That is the case for the women and men in ministry as well. Brother Geoff specifically mentions the inadequacy he feels at times and how the pandemic has heightened those feelings while on the other hand it has also affirmed who he is in ministry. When a tragic event happens, God can use that time to step in and make you uncomfortable, but in that moment also do His best work.

Reflection & the *Missio Dei*

As a church our mission is The Mission. The Father sent the Son so that the Holy Spirit could live in the Church and the Church could step out into the World to bring it back to the Father through the Holy Spirit and Son. At the core, it is all intrinsically connected. *Missio Dei* takes it even further to show the Church fundamentally what it should be doing to bring the World back to the Father.

What COIVD-19 has done to the global church is forced it to reevaluate what the true Mission is. With the majority of traveling in the United States of America and outside of it being limited, churches are now forced to look locally to do missional work. As Luke gave the

[11] Brother Geoff, personal interview, December 1, 2020.

[12] Brother Geoff, personal interview, December 1, 2020.

example, there was a time he was called out to help jump someone's vehicle. They were stuck on the side of the road, the church knew Luke had experience with vehicles and was available, so off he went to help. In other ways, Ginger, as part of a women's group, would pray for families, arrange for meals and groceries to be delivered, and assist where needed. By focusing more on the community around them, Luke, Ginger, and the Church at the Creek are starting to focus back on the root of *Missio Dei*.

As a whole, the Church at the Creek has adapted really well in a time where everything is unpredictable. For a church in rural Tennessee, they are more than likely leaps and bounds ahead of the even smaller, further out churches in their area. Having a strong pastor helps as well. Brother Geoff stepped up to the plate to find a way to provide a true Sunday morning service experience to his congregation. Luke and Ginger both mentioned that they have not watched other church's services during the pandemic, due to the fact they both really like their pastors' sermons. This can be a huge factor in how many people the videos are reaching and how people react to them. Brother Geoff has gone above and beyond in most of the videos he films in different locations to post on Sunday. The church, as a whole, is also working really hard to take into consideration all of the members and what are the best actions to keep the most people safe and healthy.

At this time, the global church is facing something it has not seen in many years. Where the church is pushed, there can sometimes come the strongest Christians and stories of faith. In this trying time, people are losing their jobs, going months without human contact or seeing their families, suicide and mental health rates are higher than ever, and it is hard to see what good can come out of it. That is where God is working and using His church to do that work. Whether it is a nurse in the COVID wing of the emergency room who prays with their patients, or a younger member of the church going to pick up groceries for an elderly or higher risk member, or the church having the ability to help pay someone's electric bill for the month and give them gift cards for groceries, God is using the small moments to have a big impact.

While living during a pandemic is not easy, sometimes a smaller town can remind you it is okay to slow down and look at the bigger picture. The congregation at the Church at the Creek has a good grasp on their purpose of loving others by showing them God's love. Perhaps the pandemic was God's way of forcing the world to readjust and realign to make sure the focus is back on Him. To take a step back and slowdown from the hustle and bustle of life to see other people and be the hands and feet that guide them.

Case Study Eight: The Wilderness can be a Time of Blessing

Leonard Bell

Leonard Bell, a retired professor of food science from Auburn University, is in his first year at Asbury Theological Seminary, pursuing a Master of Divinity degree. He and his wife live in Auburn, Alabama and have three children and three grandchildren.

Context: Suburban Central Alabama
Affiliation: United Methodist
Size: 1,200 members

Introduction

Disasters come in various forms which affect communities and their churches in various ways. Wildfires that swept through Paradise, California, destroyed over a dozen churches and thousands of other buildings in 2018. Due to evacuations that dispersed their congregants, the pastors in Paradise were challenged to provide relief to them. Yet, in the midst of the disaster, it was recognized that "the faith community is where people find belonging, they find acceptance, they find hope."[1] Similarly, Primera Iglesia Bautista Mexicana outside Dallas, Texas, was destroyed by a tornado on October 20, 2019; although their church building was gone, the congregation continued to meet at a nearby church.[2] These natural disasters were acute, happening quickly, which

[1] Shellnutt, K. (2018, Nov 16). "Paradise fire burned most church buildings, but 'the Church Is still alive.'" *Christianity Today.* https://www.christianitytoday.com/news/2018/november/paradise-california-churches-camp-firerevival.html.

[2] Manuel, O. (2019, Nov 28). "A tornado destroyed this church, but its members still feel gratitude." *The Dallas Morning News.* https://www.dallasnews.com/news/2019/11/28/a-tornado-destroyed-this-church-but-itsmembers-still-feel-gratitude/.

allowed for recovery and rebuilding to begin shortly thereafter. In early 2020, a different type of disaster happened. However, it was not an acute disaster that destroyed physical church buildings, but a long-term, chronic disaster that challenged the body of Christ around the world. A global pandemic caused by a novel coronavirus, COVID-19, shut down schools, businesses, and churches. As churches stopped holding worship services, their fate and that of the congregation were called into question. The objective of this congregational study was to examine how one suburban Methodist church in Alabama responded to the challenges of the 2020 COVID-19 pandemic.

Church Context

War Eagle United Methodist Church (WEUMC) is a suburban church in Lee County, Alabama. WEUMC is part of the Alabama-West Florida Conference of the United Methodist Church. Pastor Cameron has served as the senior pastor at WEUMC for three years and has been in ministry for over twenty years. The church is also supported by two associate pastors, as well as a pastor emeritus. Of the 1,200 primarily Caucasian members belonging to WEUMC, approximately 350 attend traditional worship services each Sunday.

Lee County is located in central Alabama on the eastern border with Georgia. Its population is approximately 164,000.[3] The first coronavirus case in Lee County occurred on March 15, 2020; over the next four to eight weeks, cumulative cases increased to 236, and then 425.[4] At the same time, COVID-19 cases in Alabama increased from 3,583 on April 12 to 9,889 on May 10.[5] As of December 1, 2020, there were 7,872 cumulative positive and presumed positive COVID-19 cases in Lee County,[6] representing 4.8 percent of the county's population.

On March 3, 2020, the federal government provided guidance entitled "30 Days to Slow the Spread," which suggested limiting groups

[3] "QuickFacts - Lee County, Alabama" United States. United States Census Bureau. https://www.census.gov/quickfacts/fact/table/leecountyalabama,US/PST045219.

[4] Lee County COVID-19 Cases. Bama Tracker: Alabama COVID-19 Tracking. https://bamatracker.com/county/Lee.

[5] Alabama COVID-19 Tracking. https://bamatracker.com/.

[6] "Lee County COVID-19 Cases." Bama Tracker: Alabama COVID-19 Tracking. https://bamatracker.com/county/Lee.

to less than ten people, while leaving the development of formal policies to state governors.[7] During a March 13 press conference with Alabama Governor Kay Ivey, State Health Officer Dr. Scott Harris suggested limiting group gatherings to less than 500 people.[8] On March 16, Bishop David Graves of the Alabama-West Florida United Methodist Conference strongly advised churches to postpone in-person worship services.[9] By March 19, gatherings of over twenty-five people were prohibited by Governor Ivey.[10] Within this framework, WEUMC held their last in-person worship service on March 8. Based on recommendations from the church staff, the church's COVID task force, and the local health department, it was quickly determined that the safest decision was to switch to an online worship format. Although not yet officially required, WEUMC held a joint online worship service on March 15 with another church at their invitation. Shortly thereafter, both Bishop Graves pressed for postponement of in-person worship and Governor Ivey banned large gatherings.

Church Response & Social Media

WEUMC conducted two traditional in-person worship services at 8:30 and 11:00 AM prior to the pandemic. Their only online media presence involved the posting of sermons on the church website. Worship services were not live-streamed or posted in their entirety. WEUMC lacked the expertise to produce online worship services. With the necessity to switch to an online worship format, but without expertise in media production, Pastor Cameron quickly hired a young man with skills in this area. WEUMC held their first independent online worship

---

[7] "30 Days to Slow the Spread." POTUS-Coronavirus-Guidelines_30-DAYS. https://www.whitehouse.gov/wpcontent/uploads/2020/03/03.16.20_coronavirus-guidance_8.5x11_315PM.pdf.

[8] "Governor Ivey Releases Statement on Alabama's First Confirmed Coronavirus Case." The Office of Alabama Governor Kay Ivey. https://governor.alabama.gov/newsroom/2020/03/governor-ivey-releases-statement-onalabamas-first-confirmed-coronavirus-case/.

[9] Graves, D.W. (2020, March 16). "An Important Word from Bishop Graves: Coronavirus Outbreak Guidance." Alabama-West Florida United Methodist Church Conference. https://www.awfumc.org/newsdetail/13526829.

[10] "Governor Ivey Issues Statement on Statewide Public Health Order." The Office of Alabama Governor Kay Ivey. https://governor.alabama.gov/newsroom/2020/03/governor-ivey-issues-statement-on-statewide-public-healthorder/.

service on March 22. The weekly online worship service, streamed Sunday at 9:30 AM, was accessible through two social media platforms: Vimeo and Facebook. In addition, online devotions and prayers were available throughout the week. Thus, WEUMC expanded their online presence from virtually nothing before the pandemic to include worship services, devotions, and prayers during the pandemic.

Despite utilizing an online format, the pastoral team worked hard to maintain the feeling of the traditional worship service. The sanctuary was a frequent setting for portions of the service. The processional hymn was a familiar Methodist hymn accompanied by the organ. Clergy wore their robes most of the time. The Apostle's Creed and Lord's Prayer were recited every Sunday. Services concluded with either an organ or piano postlude. So, the general structuring of the online service preserved the tone of traditional worship.

Four online worship services were examined to understand the types of messages being presented to parishioners during the pandemic. These included April 2, 2020 (Easter Sunday) and the following three Sundays.

The Easter Sunday service opened with a melancholy acapella solo of "Were You There (When They Crucified my Lord)" while the video remained focused on the sanctuary altar and cross. The tone quickly changed as the pastor greeted the congregation with "Christ is Risen!" Ten demographically different church families responded through video clips with "He is risen indeed!" These proclamations were followed by a previously-recorded stirring rendition of the traditional Easter processional hymn, "Christ the Lord is Risen Today." The morning prayer and offertory prayer made vague references to health challenges, strange times, and ministry looking different, but no actual mention of the pandemic occurred. The morning prayer emphasized the good news of the resurrection, stated nothing is bigger than God, and urged congregants to live as Easter people.

The Easter sermon focused on Matthew 28:1-10. Pastor Cameron began by describing the differences between past fancy, fanfare-filled Easter mornings and the current situation of worshiping apart. Alabama citizens were in lockdown, restricted to their homes amidst the uncertainty of the pandemic. Thus, Easter in 2020 was more representative and realistic to that first Easter when the disciples were grieving and huddled with fear inside their homes. The disciples were feeling many of the same feelings as the congregants on this day. The women went to the tomb out of obligation, but encountered an angel who told them Jesus had risen.

Returning to the disciples with fear and joy, Jesus met the women and told them not to be afraid. Pastor Cameron indicated that the congregation's response should be similar – encountering Christ brings joy. Love wins over sin and death. Referring back to the current state of separation, the pastor said that Christ does not need fancy church services and fanfare. The Good News can be proclaimed through the lives and testimony of the congregants. Church members are to go into the world, without fear and filled with joy, to share the good news of Jesus Christ. The service then jubilantly concluded with the "Hallelujah Chorus" from Handel's Messiah.

The tone of the Easter service, as a whole, transitioned from somber to joyous. The sermon, likewise, started somber, but ended with a message of joy. Nowhere in the Easter service was COVID-19 or the pandemic mentioned. When questioned about its absence, Pastor Cameron passionately expressed how Easter is a time for good news. Congregants are bombarded with bad news during the other six days of the week. So, the focus of Easter was on hope, joy, new life, and the resurrection. Easter was not to be a time of mourning. Despite being separated by the pandemic, this message of hope found in Christ was clearly presented through the online Easter service.

The April 19 service began with the lighting of a candle to represent Christ as the light of the world. A quartet of singers led the uplifting opening hymn, "Crown Him with Many Crowns." The morning prayer gave thanks for the power of the resurrection that is no match for the powers of evil, but did not explicitly mention the pandemic. The sermon was based on Psalm 23. Reading Psalm 23 can give peace and calmness during these difficult times associated with of the virus, its pandemic, quarantines, and separation. Faith that does not make a practical difference in handling difficult situations is not a very strong faith. Psalm 23 can change one's outlook to better handle life's difficulties.

The sermon was developed to show how the good shepherd of Psalm 23 brings peace, restoration, wisdom, courage, hope, companionship, strength, protection, healing, abundance, goodness, and mercy. The service ended with "Hymn of Promise," which contains a message of hope, comfort, and renewal. Unlike last week's service, an explicit, albeit brief, reference to the pandemic was made during the sermon. Consistent with the Easter service, the distinct message of hope and comfort was effectively delivered through the sermon and hymns.

After two services with minimal references to the pandemic, the online worship service on April 26 placed it at the forefront. From April 12 to April 26, the number of COVID-19 cases in Lee County increased by over fifty percent from 236 cases to 365 cases.[11] The service began with the proclamation, "This is the day that the Lord has made, let us rejoice and be glad in it!" The opening hymn, "Easter People, Raise Your Voices," followed with a spirit of exaltation. The anthem was a bluegrass rendition of "In the Garden," which describes the joy of personally experiencing Christ's presence as "he walks with me, and he talks with me."[12] The sermon was based on the Emmaus story found in Luke 24:13-35. Pastor Cameron began by exclaiming that ministry in the midst of a pandemic was very different. One never knew the challenges that each day would hold – providing money for power bills, dealing with food insecurity, helping teenagers grow through socially-distanced ministries, or conducting limited-attendance funerals. During their walk to Emmaus, the disciples did not recognize Jesus was walking with them. In the shock and trauma of the pandemic accompanied by feelings of isolation, grief, worry, and fear, it is critical to remember that Jesus is walking with us. He promises to bring us peace and joy. He is our hope and comfort. A trio concluded the service appropriately by singing "I Am Not Alone," that shares "in the midst of deep sorrow" and "the dark of night … I will not fear" because "I am not alone."[13] Christ is with us. Like the previous two weeks, the theme of Christ's presence providing hope and comfort radiated from the service.

---

[11] Lee County COVID-19 Cases. Bama Tracker: Alabama COVID-19 Tracking. https://bamatracker.com/county/Lee.

[12] Charles Austin Miles. "In the garden" In *The United Methodist hymnal: book of United Methodist worship* (United Methodist Publishing House, 1989), 314.

[13] Kari Jobe - "I Am Not Alone" SongLyrics. http://www.songlyrics.com/kari-jobe/i-am-not-alone-lyrics/.

One additional observation must be noted regarding the April 26 service. In the middle of the sermon, Pastor Cameron paused to conduct a video chat with the local hospital's chaplain. This conversation placed additional emphasis on the growing pandemic beyond the sermon's message. The chaplain described the stressful hospital environment, resulting from the pandemic. Yet, images of hope have simultaneously emerged in the form of flashing car lights during an evening park and pray community event, hero banners displayed around the hospital, and staff compassion expressed for isolated patients. Christ can be seen in the middle of the pandemic. When asked what the church family could do to help, the chaplain's response was to stay home, wear a mask, use hand sanitizer, maintain social distancing, and do not push to return to normal too soon, or the virus will surge. This message from April 26, 2020 foreshadowed the future grim reality. New COVID-19 cases within the United States were decreasing in late May, averaging around 20,000 per day, but surged to over 200,000 new cases per day by the second week of December.[14] People nationwide failed to take the pandemic seriously.

The online worship service from May 3 again began with the pastor's exuberant greeting, "This is the day that the Lord has made, let us rejoice and be glad in it!" As the season of Easter continued, WEUMC prayed congregants encounter the risen Christ. Rejoicing in the presence of the living Christ was expressed through the opening hymn, "He Lives." Unlike the previous three weeks, the morning prayer specifically referred to those sick with COVID-19 and prayed for its elimination from the world. The sermon message was developed around the story of Thomas questioning the resurrection of Jesus in John 20:24-29. Thomas doubted and was unsure. He sought proof. However, Thomas did not actually need to touch the wounded hands of Jesus. Once he saw Christ offering himself, Thomas simply responded "My Lord and My God." In these strange times, church members were perhaps experiencing doubt and wondered where God was. However, Jesus remains available to everyone. Our problems can be brought to Christ. The Christian faith is about trust. That faith can be demonstrated by responding like Thomas. The church's foundation is not uncertainty but Jesus Christ. The service

[14] "Trends in Number of COVID-19 Cases and Deaths in the US Reported to CDC, by State/Territory. Coronavirus Disease 2019 (COVID-19)." Center for Disease Control and Prevention. https://covid.cdc.gov/covid-datatracker/#trends_dailytrendscases.

ended with a duet of "The Church's One Foundation." Like the other three services examined, the underlying message of hope and joy found in Jesus was apparent.

Pastoral Approach

One way to evaluate the theology of a church and its pastor is by the messages conveyed through the worship services. During the four online services, the sermons and music portrayed a common thread of hope and joy in the resurrected Christ who is present with us. Jesus walks with us in our difficulties. Comfort can be found in Him. This theological message was important for congregants who were experiencing the common hardship of the pandemic and the associated lockdown, which prevented them from being able to directly interact with each other or the pastoral staff.

Pastor Cameron shared some additional theological perspectives about the pandemic. COVID-19 has caused an unknown future. Answers do not exist. Many aspects of life are out of our control. The scary, uncertain, bewildering current times can be viewed as a type of spiritual wilderness. Today's Christians are wandering in this wilderness, much like the ancient Israelis. However, the wilderness can be a time of blessing. God's provision can be better understood. He is providing if we can identify it. American Christians can learn patience. Our situations teach us to wait on, and trust in, the Lord. God is still God in the wilderness. God draws us closer in times of trouble. As we live as God's family, He will not leave us. God is with us; hope and joy are waiting. The Christian witness will be stronger from the challenges encountered with COVID-19. Although "wilderness" was not an explicit component of the sermons, the loving presence of God drawing us close to comfort us was constantly conveyed during worship.

When asked about ministering to the congregation, Pastor Cameron sighed and described the challenges of providing congregational care during the pandemic. The Lee County COVID-19 rate was less than 5 percent on December 1, as mentioned previously. However, the rate within WEUMC was already over 10 percent by early November. Thus, a lot of time was spent ministering to individuals afflicted with the virus and their families. Some congregants have been angry and embarrassed that they or their family member became ill with the virus after saying it was not a big deal. As hospitals completely restricted visitation, comforting the families who could not be with their hospitalized loved one was hard. The church also had congregants who were experiencing dismay from transmitting the virus to others. Marriages that were in trouble before the pandemic were now worse. People experienced a lot of guilt and fear. As a result, pastoral care typically involved 5 hours of phone calls per day by the pastor and associate pastors.

Communication efforts with the congregation increased by both email and phone. The use of email was the primary mode of communication, in an attempt to keep church members engaged. Announcements, newsletters, and links to devotions were provided electronically. Some announcements were posted on Facebook. WEUMC also started a phone ministry that has continued. Volunteers were assigned 15-20 people to check on by phone. Initially, all church members were called daily, but the frequency was lowered to weekly and now every two weeks. The phone ministry provided congregants with real verbal conversation while getting them temporarily away from their computer and smart phone screens. The pastoral staff would then follow up with congregants who expressed deeper needs to the phone ministry volunteers.

The use of Zoom, a web-based platform for video conferencing, enabled a wide variety of interactive church gatherings. Sunday School classes and Bible studies were held using Zoom. Although the technology was available, not all Sunday School classes opted to meet virtually. Youth groups and choirs also met using Zoom. WEUMC continued to provide discipleship opportunities virtually as well. The virtual format allowed these groups to meet at flexible times that were not restricted to the traditional in-person scheduling of the church.

Recognizing the need for in-person activities in a socially-distanced manner, the staff offered a variety of drive-through celebrations at the church. Communion was provided using a drive-through format. On Palm Sunday, staff waved palm branches as congregants drove through the church parking lot. Confirmation and graduations were celebrated in a similar manner. WEUMC also enclosed an outdoor greenspace where additional socially-distanced events could be held.

Children's activities, college activities, and family ministry events were offered outside, but still required masks to be worn.

Pastor Cameron indicated that worshiping and ministering from a distance was frustrating because of the difficulty in "reading" the congregation. Behaviors, or lack of behaviors, can be misinterpreted, leading to paranoia that the church was not meeting a particular need. Two areas of concern involved whether or not adequate discipleship opportunities existed for congregants, as well as whether the exclusively online church existence was satisfying the desire for community and fellowship. Although the church should be providing these, it was also the church's responsibility not to put congregants in peril. Many of the people who desired more active participation were those most vulnerable to serious or fatal outcomes from the virus.

With a serious tone, Pastor Cameron confessed that "it is a hard time to be clergy; nobody goes into this to be a televangelist." Being away from your people is hard. Seminary did not prepare clergy to minister under these conditions. WEUMC contained a few chronically irritable congregants who wore on the patience of the pastoral staff. These people were responding to trauma, lacked patience with life being hard, and feared job loss. They felt more comfortable venting to the pastors rather than their family, friends, or work colleagues. Overall, the never-ending pandemic was exhausting for the pastoral staff. The increasingly stressful situation led to a sincere concern about pastoral mental health. Pastor Cameron observed other pastors in the area were experiencing fatigue and burnout from the prolonged crisis. The pastors themselves needed pastoral care.

The ministerial goal of WEUMC in the midst of the pandemic was to promote safety and minimize risk while keeping congregants connected and discipled. From online worship services to expanded church communication to individual ministries via Zoom, everything has been reworked and changed which has been both exhausting and exhilarating for the pastoral staff.

Congregational Response

Four Caucasian congregants between 60 and 80 years of age were interviewed to gain their perspectives regarding the pandemic, God, and the church. Two males (Bill and Chris) and two females (Beth and Julia) shared their insights. Of the four congregants, three watched every online worship service and the fourth watched approximately 70 percent of them.

None of these congregants believed God played a role in the pandemic. Bill indicated God was aware of the pandemic and could intercede if He chose. He prayed for God to control the pandemic but knew God did not always intercede in the natural world. Chris expressed he was more aware of God's presence during the day, especially during his devotional study time. Beth said that God reminded her that He was in control and believed that His protection would surround her family. She indicated her relationship with God had strengthened. Likewise, Julia felt the pandemic brought her closer to God and helped her recognize He was in control. Overall, these congregants did not show resentment toward God about the pandemic and expressed an unwavering faith.

The congregants were asked about their worship experiences during the pandemic. All four congregants were generally complimentary regarding the transition to online worship services. Bill responded that limitations in resources and expertise were overcome to produce quality online services. Chris added that the pastoral staff was effective at incorporating other people into the service. Beth commented that the "pastors did an incredible job of adapting to online services!" Although online services received favorable reviews, all four congregants expressed their dismay with the lack of in-person fellowship. Bill noted the importance of the social aspects – hugging, hand-shaking, watching people worship, speaking with friends. Chris concurred about the frustration of not being able to socialize with friends and worship together. Both Beth and Julia also missed worshiping with friends in the sanctuary. This social aspect of in-person worship stood out as a significant deficiency with online worship services.

Pastor Cameron noted that congregants became more actively involved in supporting the church's virtual ministries. A large variety of people participated in worship services, especially musicians. Children, youth, college students, and families also helped with different aspects of worship. Congregants led online devotions and prayers. Volunteers emerged to participate in the previously described phone ministry. Church members were anxious to help.

After six months of no in-person worship, the first opportunity for the congregation to return was September 27. Two in-person "practice" services were held first for church staff and the COVID task force and then for the larger Board of Stewards on September 13 and 20, respectively. These services allowed WEUMC to work out details for safety and hospitality before allowing the congregation to return. WEUMC offered limited capacity worship services at 8:30 and 11:00 AM on Sundays. People were required to register to attend. The sanctuary holds around 350 people so capacity was reduced to around 80 people, or 25 percent, to allow for six-foot social distancing between families. WEUMC followed the guidelines for starting back provided by the Alabama-West Florida United Methodist Conference. In preparation for the anticipated higher demand during Advent, an additional 9:45 AM service was added on

December 6, to accommodate more people, while being able to spread them out more effectively. This service was viewed as a "temporary bridge to normalcy," and will be removed once the attendance restrictions end. As part of returning to in-person services, masks were required in church buildings. Mask wearing was a controversial topic because not all local churches required them. Hand sanitizer was provided. The choir sang in masks from the balcony, spaced apart. The structuring and requirements associated with the in-person worship were implemented so that congregants could return safely to an exciting, spiritual, hope-filled church life.

Of the four congregants interviewed, two have returned to attending in-person services and two have not. Bill and Julia have not attended the in-person service due to lack of comfort with large groups, as well as family health considerations. Chris attended immediately and expressed his frustration that WEUMC stayed closed so long. He was never uncomfortable about the pandemic. Beth expressed concern about returning to church, having survived COVID-19 herself, but decided to try the first available in-person service. She was impressed with the measures taken to promote safety and continued to attend every Sunday morning.

Post-Pandemic Future

Despite COVID-19 cases surging in December 2020, the pandemic will eventually come to an end, and the church will experience its lasting effects. For WEUMC, the most obvious impact will be the continuation of a pre-recorded online worship service streamed Sunday mornings at 9:30 AM. This service reached individuals who otherwise were not attending church. Pastor Cameron and the four congregants were also asked their opinions about additional effects of the pandemic on the church.

Bill said that returning to "normal" will take a long time. By normal, he was primarily referring to a full sanctuary for worship. He further noted how the pastoral staff solicited feedback from the congregation during the pandemic, which would likely continue after the pandemic. Chris expected that once restrictions are removed (i.e., no masks, no social distancing) the in-person worship services will be full. He also stated that the church has a major opportunity to share the stories about how the church kept going, the congregational care provided, and where God appeared in the midst of the pandemic. Beth thought the church would emerge stronger. WEUMC learned to be creative and adapt to the difficult situation. The pandemic forced congregants to explore new ways to stay connected. Julia added how the online services expanded its availability to more people.

Pastor Cameron explained that the pandemic allowed WEUMC the freedom to experiment, adapt, innovate, and do trial runs of new ideas. It has been an "opportunity to rebound to a better normal." Consistent with a resurrection mentality, some activities or ministries may die off, while others will be reborn in new and exciting ways. The chancel choir has been a constant component of worship for decades, but through the pandemic, the church experienced new musical styles (e.g., youth, college, blue grass, contemporary duets) that were infused into the online worship services. It has been an opportunity to revitalize worship services, as new worship leaders and participants emerged.

However, the church is not only about worship. The goal of WEUMC is to enable growth along the Christian journey throughout life. Pastor Cameron stated, "We get the opportunity to take the best of who we are into the future. So, what's the core of who we are and how do we get to bring that into the future?" Through the pandemic, the pastor identified those core aspects to be discipleship, pastoral care, worship, and service. WEUMC discovered new opportunities in these areas. The church will be able to evaluate and remove ineffective ministries and get back to the basic ways of expressing and growing their faith. The prospect of rebirth was exciting to Pastor Cameron.

Reflections & the *Missio Dei*

God works through the church to transform both His people and creation for growing and strengthening the Kingdom of God; this concept is known as the *Missio Dei*. Broadly speaking, the *Missio Dei* includes both the verbal proclamation of the Good News and actively demonstrating neighborly love through tangible service. Although the pandemic prevented in-person worship and restricted gatherings, WEUMC was able to continue their participation within the *Missio Dei*, as demonstrated by their consistent community outreach.

The primary outreach activity of WEUMC has been food distribution to food insecure families. This ministry continued strong, despite the pandemic. Because elementary schools were not meeting in-person in the spring, one food distribution ministry switched from sending food to the school to actually delivering the food to the needy families at home. The church also staffed a drive-through food distribution site at a local high school. Chris, who was involved with food distribution, reported that during 17 weeks, the WEUMC food ministry engaged over 160 volunteers to serve over 900 families with 54,000 pounds of food. He continued that there was an intentional effort for WEUMC to be the church outside of the church during the pandemic.

Information about the outreach activities of WEUMC was blended into the online worship services. On Easter, the offertory prayer made reference to being thankful for church members who continued to bear witness by distributing food to needy families, writing letters to those isolated, preparing meals for health care workers, and providing videos for the church. The April 19 online service included a specific ministry moment where a church family provided an update about the food ministry. The following week's service included a ministry moment highlighting children who wrote letters and made cards for isolated senior citizens of the church. On May 3, the ministry moment described the creation of the telephone ministry and efforts of the church staff to keep the congregation connected. People saw WEUMC being the hands and feet of Jesus. Chris commented that keeping the congregation informed about the ongoing church outreach encouraged them to maintain generous giving during the pandemic. Pastor Cameron also noted that financial donations continued strong during the six months of no in-person services.

WEUMC strived to continue participating within the *Missio Dei* during the pandemic. Within the church, they nurtured the congregation by keeping in contact with and supporting isolated church members. They reached outside the church through meals for health care workers and food distribution to needy families. Through strong financial donations, some needy families were able to receive financial assistance. Some church members carefully helped with out-of-town hurricane cleanup. Members of WEUMC loved their neighbors through their actions.

In addition to the outreach displayed by WEUMC members, the pastoral staff worked hard to provide an uplifting biblically-based message through their online worship services. Congregants, as well as non-church members, viewed these services and heard the Good News. Church members volunteered to provide video devotions that remain available online. Through these continually accessible online services and devotions, WEUMC shared the Word of God.

Through the examination of four worship services, as well as interviews with Pastor Cameron and four parishioners, several important observations emerged regarding the response of War Eagle United Methodist Church to the COVID-19 pandemic. WEUMC successfully developed and presented new online worship experiences for the congregation. The topic of the pandemic did not monopolize worship, nor was it ignored. A theological perspective of God's loving presence providing joy, hope, and comfort during the trials of the pandemic was consistently presented. This message corresponds with the similar perspective expressed after the Paradise, California, wildfires that the church is where people find hope.[15]

Overall, the pastor expressed a generally positive and enthusiastic attitude. Rather than barriers, the pastor saw the challenges associated with the pandemic as opportunities for renewal. The pastoral staff worked hard to provide an upbeat message and sense of community to the congregation, despite not being able to meet in person. With a sense of frustration and concern, the pandemic's potential toll on clergy morale and mental health was articulated.

The congregants were upbeat about the church's response to the pandemic. No major complaints emerged in terms of pastoral actions, and most thought the pastors did a very good job of adapting to the online format for worship. The continuation of effective church outreach, while modified for safety, was highlighted. The unifying concern raised by this group was the lack of in-person fellowship. The group missed being able to visit with friends, see people's faces during worship, shake hands, eat together, and hug. The sense of community is a major aspect of these congregants' worship experience and church participation.

Some comparisons can be made between how churches respond to different types of disasters. The acute natural disaster most frequently results in the destruction of property. Yet, the congregation typically regroups and gathers temporarily at an alternate site until the church building is repaired or rebuilt. Congregants continue to directly interact and support each other as the body of Christ. Such was the response by Primera Iglesia Bautista Mexicana after the destructive tornado.[16] During the more chronic COVID-19 pandemic, church buildings remained intact, but they were simply unavailable. Fear about spreading the highly contagious virus with its potentially fatal outcome prevented groups from assembling. Therefore, the congregation could not regroup elsewhere and fellowship was limited to virtual gatherings online. The pastor and congregants of WEUMC tolerated the situation, but were not content.

---

[15] Shellnutt, "Paradise fire".

[16] Manuel, "A tornado destroyed this church".

This simple comparison reinforces the concept that the body of Christ is not about the physical building, but the people. Theologian Edmund Clowney stated, "When Protestants speak of going to church … they are not thinking of a building but of a congregation. The congregation, not the building, is holy."[17] Buildings come and go, but the heart and soul of the church are its interactive, relational, spirit-filled members.

---

[17] Clowney, E. (2004, June 1). "One holy catholic and apostolic church" *Tabletalk Magazine*. https://www.ligonier.org/learn/articles/one-strongholystrong-catholic-and-apostolic-church/.

Case Study Nine: If God is for us, Who can Stand Against us?

J.P. Bolick

J.P. Bolick is married with two small children, ages 3 and 7, serves as a committee member at Hinds Feet Farm, is a committee member of "Church and Society" UMC at Central United Methodist Church in Asheville(NC), helps lead various youth initiatives at his church, and is involved in the local "Walk to Emmaus" team. He is currently in Graduate School to attain his Masters of Divinity at Asbury Theological Seminary.

Context: Rural North Carolina
Affiliation: Freewill Baptist
Size: About 40 members

Introduction

I met "Kevin" and his family in the parking lot of a Mountain Golf Course in North Carolina. I had both of my sons piled on the golf cart putting in my clubs. My kids were wearing their bright orange "Jesus" trucker hats. He had his two kids and wife packed in so they could ride along while he played a round of golf. I am not sure who asked who to play together, but I think he might have initiated things by mentioning he liked my kids' hats. We then said good-bye and headed down to the first hole. We had waited on the group in front of us to hit their ball when I heard a cart driving towards the tee box. I think that might have been when I asked if they wanted to join us for the round. Either way, we greeted each other from a "socially distanced" safe space, teed off separately and headed down to our balls on the fairway.

It was only the second time I had taken the kids out to play. Kevin said it had been months since he had gotten out to play and when he asked his kids what they wanted to do, they said go to a golf course.

We made it through a few holes and during that time I learned he was a pastor, grew up in Ohio like me, and finished seminary within the last year. What are the odds? I just laughed inside. One reason I laughed is because coincidences like this have happened all the time since starting Asbury Theological Seminary. In my first semester, I invited the Holy Spirit to be a part of my entire life. Since then, I have seen the Holy Spirit create chance meetings on a regular basis. I just didn't realize this relationship with "Kevin" would lead both of us to team up for a congregational study on how the COVID pandemic has impacted his church and congregation, but it did!

I had two assignments from different classes which required pastoral interviews. One was this assignment for Missional Formation and the other was for Worship Leadership. Thankfully, when I reached out to Kevin, he was willing to help on both assignments. The following study is the direct result of our chance meeting for 18 holes of golf.

Let us begin the discussion by defining our purpose. First, I want to paint a general picture of the kind of church I studied and its congregation. Second, I will review the church's social media ministry both before and during the pandemic. Then, I will discuss the four weeks of worship services I observed. Fourth, I will examine the Pastor's approach to his ministry and theology of the pandemic. Along with this, I will explore its effect on the congregation found through congregational interviews. Fifth, I will examine the potential of the pandemic's impact on the future of this congregation. Finally, I discuss the overarching theme through all participant interviews of inner eschatological peace, freewill with respect, and trust in the Kingdom, and will reflect on how this case study personally impacted my perceptions and how I view the pandemic's overall impact on the church's *Missio Dei*.

Church Context

On my drive to see the church in person, the first thing I noticed was how rural the area was, with the typical country feel for North Carolina. When pulling up to the church I immediately noticed its large welcoming concrete steps leading into the church, the red all-brick exterior, and the white steeple on top. It appeared to be 50-70 years old and well maintained. The parking seemed adequate for the church size, and it was just a short walk to enter in the front door. I was surprised to learn the number of members was only about 25-40 people. It is very small in comparison to my experiences as a church member, but, based on the interviews, is a very closely-knit family. The worship at the church is a blend of contemporary and traditional. This style seems to make sense because the pastor is in his twenties and the church deacons are in their 60's, 70's and 80's. Moving forward, we will refer to this church as "Freewill Baptist."

The pandemic in North Carolina is tracked online using a COVID-19 County Alert System. This alert system was designed to help communities make decisions about how to slow its spread. It is a three-tiered system where each county is categorized as yellow, orange, or red, based on its level of cases as a percentage of people. Yellow indicates the county has "significant" spread of the virus, orange indicates a "substantial" spread of the virus, and red indicates a "critical" spread of the virus.[1] The church and its immediate community did not appear to be impacted at all, based on the experience of those interviewed for the study. The church's county numbers were in the yellow, or "significant" tier, and the surrounding counties were in the red, or "critical" tier. This community appears to be physically insulated from densely populated areas and, socially, does not appear to be very transient in nature.

Church Response & Social Media

Many churches in the state of North Carolina do not have an online presence. While most urban churches have an online presence, a lot of rural churches do not. My personal experience with social media and the three rural churches I have engaged with the past month has been consistent. None of the churches offered internet access in their building before the pandemic and only one, "Freewill Baptist" church in this study, had made the decision to begin online worship services and provide internet access. The other two churches were doing drive-up services using FM transmitters, but did not want internet provided at the church. One of these churches was even approached concerning internet access for their youth, who are active in Boys and Girls Scouts, and

[1] Fowler, Hayley. "Nearly Half of NC Counties Are Now in Coronavirus 'Red' Zone. Here Are the 48 Listed." *Raleigh News & Observer*, www.newsobserver.com/news/coronavirus/article247699700.html.

offered to pay the expenses but were refused by leadership. The following discussion about social media only pertains to "Freewill Baptist" church and will reveal how social media has a role in all churches, especially during a pandemic.

"Freewill Baptist" has evolved from a social media standpoint. The only presence the church had online was a sound recording of the service it posted on YouTube, which is more than they had two years prior. They are currently doing their services on Facebook Live and plan to continue providing an online service for its congregation. What facilitated the decision to be engaged in social media and provide ways for those unable to physically attend services to worship? We can dig a little deeper and see how it was a combination of events which created their online evolution. First, the COVID-19 pandemic played a major role in the church decision to use social media, because there were members who had underlying conditions which created a health risk to attend in person. Second, the state had a mandate which restricted the number of people who could gather. Finally, what impacted the decision to engage with social media was the church's newly appointed millennial pastor who is well-versed in social media, willing and able to set it up, and who recognized the value of an online presence. "Freewill Baptist" was ready for online services within weeks of the COVID-19 pandemic.

Next, we will review the church's social media ministry during the pandemic and talk about the four weeks of sermons I observed. Our focus on the observations of the worship service is two-fold. First, I want to identify basic elements of the service, such as the worship space, scripture used, musical reflections, sermon themes, and any other notable observations made. Second, and directly related to the pandemic, I will examine in detail how the COVID- 19 pandemic was addressed and expressed theologically within the worship service.

April 12, 2020

The environment of this service was interesting in several ways. First, this was a sunrise worship service, you could barely see the silhouette of the pastor. Second, when the sun began to rise, the first things you see are three wooden crosses in the background, which are symbolic of the crucifixion. Then you notice the backdrop filled with cascading mountain tops. It was a beautiful environment for this type of service. The scene matched the liturgical calendar, as well as the use of scripture, music and sermon's theme. The pastor was dressed in dark tan slacks, a pressed white shirt, pink tie, and pastel yellow jacket.

This online worship service's scripture came from John 20:1-22. As mentioned earlier, this worship service tied in nicely with the scripture, the liturgical calendar, and the sermon being about the resurrection of Christ. "Kevin," the pastor, read the scripture and pointed out how the scripture points to the changes God made from that miraculous morning. He then talks about the tomb. How it was empty, and the disciples were surprised to find Jesus missing. He mentions how they found the folded grave clothes, which was significant. He then prayed while giving thanks for salvation, asking for the sermon to be blessed, and for the people who were watching to be blessed.

The music was very uplifting, positive, hopeful and tied into the overall theme of the resurrection and Jesus being the way to salvation. The songs chosen were contemporary and included the following: *In Christ Alone, Glorious Day, It Is Finished, and Resurrecting.* The music in this service was performed by the pastor and two members. They pastor played the guitar and was the lead vocal during all songs. One notable event during the music was in the middle of the song as the wind kept blowing off the music until "Kevin" had to finally stop. All three of the people started laughing and their comfort level spoke volumes about how they did not take themselves too seriously. Eventually the wind settled down and they gracefully continued worship. One additional observation I would like to note about the music was how they seemed to be slightly closer than the suggested 6-foot mark set for social distancing, but they did maintain a 4-5 ft space during the music set.

The sermon theme encompassed the day's theme of the change experienced in the resurrection, as well as the scripture reading and music which supported it. During the scripture reading, the pastor mentioned how God made changes that miraculous morning. He tells the story about how it was a custom to throw your napkin down after finishing a meal, and the only time you would fold a napkin is when you were planning to come back to the table and eat. He then talks about how the grave clothes in Jesus' tomb were found folded, and how it symbolizes

Jesus signaling his return and resurrection. The pastor discussed how God was so eternal that even in his death, he left a message of how he was coming back. He mentions how Jesus went from being missing, to the message, and finally to the master. He brings up how Jesus is our hope and how thankful he is for what Jesus did at the Cross. It was a message of thankfulness and hope because of Jesus Christ.

It is important to note some detail about how the COVID-19 pandemic was addressed and expressed theologically within the worship service. "Kevin" tied in the pandemic by sharing a story about the past week. He had been doing his daily devotions at the same place the sunrise service was currently taking place. "Kevin" mentioned that everyone should think about Jesus at every sunrise, and how it symbolizes the resurrection and hope. He mentioned how his car did not start one morning at devotions, and he had to call an automotive technician to replace the starter. He then talked about how we can face surprises, like our car not starting, bad days, and bad viruses much easier by knowing that Jesus has risen. Theologically, it appears he obviously is concerned with the pandemic, because the service is conducted outside. He also expressed the thought that if it is his time to go home to heaven, it's his time. He did not give any indication that the pandemic is God passing his judgement on the world. He encouraged everyone to do what God lays on their heart. If staying home is what they feel God calls them to do, they should do it and feel good about it. He believes some people are led to do only online worship and he encouraged them to do that unashamedly. He said he believes God said to spread out and be wise. He discussed how God will let them know what they need to do concerning the pandemic, and that while we have a reason to be fearful, there is hope because of the resurrection. He mentioned how some people misuse scripture, like saying the disciples were quarantined in the Upper Room, but they were quarantined because they were terrified of the Jewish leaders who had just killed Jesus. He reiterated how everyone should do what they feel God wants of them, and praise Jesus in the process. He noted that evil reigns pervasively in the middle of God's kingdom, but Jesus wants to sustain us amid our fear and anxiety. The entire time he addressed the pandemic, he exuded hope, love, and respect for the decisions of others.

April 19, 2020

The space for this service was interesting in several ways. First, it was filmed inside the church. The church has hard wood floors, a stained-glass window illuminated in the background, a United States flag on the left, and what looks like a State Flag on the right, with two wooden chairs between the two flags. The pastor used a metal stand as his pulpit and music sheet stand. There is also a television set above the stained-glass, which is not visible on the video, except in the very beginning. The pastor was dressed comfortably in khakis and a dark sweater and dressy tennis shoes.

This online worship service's scripture came from Luke 21: 1-26. The pastor began by saying how following scripture is simple. People can make it seem so difficult but it is really so easy in theory. He noted that you do not have to ask questions of scripture all of the time. Sometimes, we can just say, "yes, sir" and, "because I love you, I will do what we are supposed to do." He mentioned the sermon title is going to be "In Case You Forgot." Again, he stated how we gather together with music and scripture to worship God, and then opened with a prayer of thanks. The scripture is about Paul's experience in Tyre, where he was warned not to go to Jerusalem. The pastor immediately transitions to the sermon.

The music is contemporary, and the pastor played it on his guitar and sang with another person standing beside him. They appear to be closer than six feet. The first song they play is *How Great is Our God.* When they finish, he immediately started to talk about how the next song might not be a popular radio song, but it is popular with him because it came directly from scripture. He emphasized how music is fun, but it is not the point of church. He says the point of church is to worship God. A notable observation during this song was that in the middle of the song they start laughing so hard that the lady just sits down. It was really endearing, because you can tell by the body language that the relationship was very friendly and peaceful, even though they kept losing their place. After this momentary break, the song is finished without a hitch. When it is over, the pastor transitions immediately into prayer and says thank you to God. He then mentions how the music did not appear on the television, which is not visible on the video.

The sermon title was "In Case You Forgot." The video actually cuts off the top of his head. The pastor starts talking about how a man tells Paul the Holy Spirit told them not to go to Jerusalem, because Paul is going to be captured or die. Paul was called through the Holy Spirit to go to the Gentiles, and was given power and gifts by the Holy Spirit. The pastor wants to make sure everyone realizes it is not about the people; it is about God working through these people. The message turns and becomes about how the deacons, like Phillip, are called to go out, as he did with the eunuch. The pastor then calls out a deacon in one of the pews named Steve, and tells him he is supposed to share the word and preach sermons. He says everyone is called to share the word, and all the people in the Bible are just ordinary, normal people. None of them are special, except Jesus. But the Holy Spirit is special, and sometimes, God works through people to accomplish special things. If someone brings up something which conflicts with what he understands of God's will, then he will immediately go to God. If God tells him to stay, he will stay, if God tells him to leave, he will leave. You cannot be persuaded by others; you must go directly to the source: God, and ask for his will to be done. He says if someone disagrees with him, it is perfectly fine. It is okay to have disagreements, and does not mean we have to get upset. Those people who told Paul not to go did not get mad at Paul, they cried because they cared about him. After consulting God, Paul heads onward to Jerusalem. The pastor then goes into how these specific Jews were wrong about circumcision, because it was not meant to be a way for salvation. He then talks about how more than 400 laws for the Jews developed from only 10 commandments. While Paul is in Jerusalem, he follows the laws to show them he cares, but he also gently tries to help them see they are being too legalistic. I struggled a little following the sermon theme of "In Case You Forgot," but the pastor ends with a prayer stating how God desires us to learn and seek knowledge.

"Kevin" did not specifically mention the pandemic this week, but he did encourage the audience to seek God when making decisions and go where the Spirit leads you. If that means to go out and do something, then you should do it. You should even do it in the face of enemies and potential harm. This is the only time when he says anything possibly alluding to the pandemic.

April 26, 2020

The worship space for this service was very similar to the April 19, 2020 service. It was filmed inside the church, but was not illuminated. My first instinct was to check out the timestamp of the service. It was 11 a.m. The pastor was dressed comfortably in blue pants, a purple sweater and casual camel-colored shoes. It looks like he recently had a haircut. The video was positioned so that it slightly cut off the top of his head.

This scripture was from Acts 22, and was a continuation from last Sunday. He reads through the scripture and it was hard to tell where the scripture reading ended and the sermon began. The sermon focused on how we do not need to defend ourselves, but we are called to defend God and the Gospel.

The music was contemporary, and the pastor had his guitar and was by himself on this day. He immediately mentioned how he cannot wait for the praise team to be back and gave many compliments on how much he appreciates them. "Kevin" then announced that they will be singing *Your Grace is Enough* and *I can only Imagine.* He called out someone by name, either in the pews or worshipping online, and mentioned how he knows they love the song I can only Imagine and he is looking forward to singing it. He then sang *Your Grace is Enough*, and at the end of the song, he immediately emphasized that grace is enough, and Jesus is all we need. The next song is announced as *I can only Imagine* and "Kevin" gets particularly emotional when talking about seeing his heavenly Father. This discussion triggered memories of his earthly father who had passed. He is both tearful and joyful at the same time. He noted the song should be called *We Can't Even Imagine* because in an eschatological sense, no matter how great we think it might be, in the end, the Kingdom of God will be much greater. The song is sung and when it is finished, he reiterated how we will not even know how great it is going to be. Through his tears, he said in the first bit of eternity it will not be his Dad that he wants to see, it will be Jesus, and he will be bowing at the foot of Jesus. It might even be undignified in how fervently he will worship Jesus.

The sermon theme was "Christians have trials, don't defend yourself, but defend the Gospel." Paul came to obey the law and was just trying to help the Jews understand that it is not the law which saves you, but forgiveness through Christ which saves. He was tried in the Jewish court of public opinion. Even though it was difficult, he never made the trial about himself. In the Old Testament, it is the same with Joseph. He never tried to defend himself. The pastor then spoke about how social media can bring out times we want to defend ourselves, but there is no reason to defend yourself. The only time you need to defend yourself is when it comes to the Gospel. The only reason Paul was in the temple for six days was to demonstrate his cleansing to his people after being among Gentiles. Unfortunately, he is grabbed in the temple and the people were about to kill him. They beat him until a centurion steps in and stops it. He takes Paul to jail where he says Paul can speak. Paul says: "I am a man which is a Jew born of Tarsus and was zealous toward God. Binding(jailing) people, men, and women. I was going to Damascus to arrest more." Then he reprises his testimony. He did not defend himself; he testified. The point is that it may come to a point in your life where the only thing you can do is share your testimony. Do not defend your testimony, just tell it. That's what Paul did. When given the opportunity came to defend himself in front of the Pharisees, Sadducees, and the council, he shared his testimony and poured out his soul instead. They do not seem to care. Some people wonder if Paul was sent to only convert the Gentiles and might have been forcing himself on the Jews by not heeding the warning of others in Tyre. The pastor resumed by sharing how Paul never made it through the ordeal and was ultimately beheaded in Rome. He made the point that there is not always a happy ending for Christians, in a physical sense. In a spiritual sense, though, because of Jesus, we always have a happy ending. The pastor then noted that he does not love God for keeping him physically healthy on earth. He talks about how Uriah was innocent while David took his wife, and Uriah died an innocent man. People need to understand that life does not get easier by being a Christian, we might not make it through physically, but we need to be prepared spiritually for God's Kingdom.

During the sermon, the pastor mentioned that if he gets COVID-19 while being mindful and carefully witnessing to people, he is not worried about dying. However, he does encourage everyone to be careful and use precautions. He noted to not let the idea of getting it make you fearful, because through Jesus, we are delivered to the Kingdom. The music reflected how a relationship with Jesus is enough, and how, in death, we cannot even begin to fathom the incredible awesomeness of being with God. His theology on the pandemic is to be careful, but not to worry about dying, because even though we die physically on earth, we live on because of Jesus.

May 3, 2020

The worship space has not changed since the April 26, 2020 service. The camera angle is better, and the top of his head is not cut off. He is wearing light blue pants, a white shirt, and a dark blazer with camel-colored dress shoes. There is a red bible or hymnal in one of the wooden chairs today. The bottom of the television is exposed in the video today, and makes me wonder if it would be nice to see the lyrics on the screen and be able to sing along from home.

The scripture of the day is Acts 23. He noted in some pre-sermon comments that he was going to read the entire scripture, and asked the entire congregation to stand. He wanted everyone to respond however they felt led to respond. He literally took the Bible off the chair and read the scripture. This was the longest reading of all four services, and he read it very quickly. When he finished, you could hear some people in the background celebrating.

The music was a blend of contemporary and traditional. The pastor was alone, playing his guitar, and singing, but I could hear more voices on the audio today than the last three services. The first song was *Wonderful Maker*. The song is kind-hearted and focused on how wonderful God is. They announced they were using Lifeway for online offerings and that they were going to have normal service and Sunday school on May 10th for Mother's Day. But the pastor remained very open-minded and kind to both the people who want to worship in person and those who feel led to stay home. The music reflected his humble, kind-hearted approach and that the main focus needs to be on God. The second song played was *Old Rugged Cross*. This is the first time I have noticed that he did not have a story to share about the song. He moved swiftly into the sermon.

The sermon theme was "If God is for Us, Who Can Be Against Us." Our past cannot be held against us. Did Paul say he was perfect?

Actually, he said he is the opposite, he says he is a murderer. The pastor said the past cannot be used against us because of the righteousness of Christ. There is nothing we can do to lose our salvation. We are clean only under the blood of Jesus (but only if God is for us). Self-righteousness and self-holiness cannot stop us from going to heaven, I cannot stop God in me, if God is for me. Paul's own religiousness and zealousness could not get in the way, Jesus came to Paul on his way to Damascus and changed his life. The Pharisees hated Christians so much they changed the law and did things to Christians that was outside of the law. Neither Jesus nor Paul were guilty of breaking the law. The Jewish leaders broke the law to kill Christians. The pastor urged that we should not be afraid to lose for God's glory. Do not worry about defending yourself (Jesus has already defended us before God). Paul led many people to Jesus while he was in prison and under house arrest. He made a bad situation good. Paul's experience is a perfect example of how Satan wins 100% of the time unless Jesus Christ intervenes. If God is for us, no one can be against us.

During the service "Kevin" mentioned the pandemic a couple of times. He mentioned the following: "Livestream will continue, and no one should feel pressured to come to the Mother's Day service. You are not going against God, or the Bible, or failing in your Christian responsibilities by staying home. Do not let someone make you feel like you must come unless God directs you so you feel you should. One deacon will not be attending because of underlying health issues, so do not feel like you need to come to the service." During another part of the service, he congratulated the upcoming graduates and mentioned he was sorry everything had not gone the way they really wanted it to (due to COVID).

Pastoral Approach

During the congregational study I sat down with the pastor and two active members from "Freewill Baptist" Church. The pastor was new to ministry and this was his first assignment. Greta was a member of the worship team and active in the worship service, and in outreach and meeting congregational members needs as well (called OutReach and InReach respectively). Tristen was a deacon and very active in the audio and visual recordings of their YouTube and Facebook ministries. The purpose of the interviews was to find out how the pandemic impacted online worship, physical worship, their view of God's role in the world, and their church's future. The congregational members also shared their thoughts on the pastor's response.

Pastor "Kevin" Interview

While interviewing the pastor, I touched on a broad list of subjects concerning the church and the pandemic. The pastor commented that the church had many older members, and that some family members made nasty accusations about how the church leaders were planning to do the services. They made the decision, as a group, to allow individuals to make their own decisions concerning attendance. One of the at-risk deacons suggested to have an online service and even volunteered to pay for the first three months of internet for the church. This was how the decision to do an online service began. Now it is a standard operating procedure for the church and will remain part of the worship service because it is being actively used and has generated positive feedback. He said his church never stopped having physical services, but added the option for online attendance via Facebook Live the second week of April, and recently almost all of the Sunday morning worship crowd is back. However, they have not returned to using the Sunday school classrooms, and the midweek Bible study is almost completely attended online. Along with these, they hope to be able to resume home meetings, Sunday School classes, and bible studies in the future.

We then had a conversation about the long-term effects of the pandemic, how the church worships, and the ministry developed to meet the congregation's needs. Long term, most of what the pastor felt is that the pandemic's effects will be bad. He hoped not, but thinks Christians, as a whole, have set a poor precedent for the future on how we handle difficulties in the world. He loved the idea of more home church worship, but we have not seen that happening, by and large. He mentioned that Barna's studies have shown how poorly it is going right now. This certainly does not make him worry, because God is in control and he knows what is best and what will happen. He reiterated again how he believes it will make the true believers remember how precious gathering truly is and see changes for the good to include a fresh desire for gathering, an online presence, and the realization of how blessed we were and are to be able to gather together. Some changes for the bad included couples who have left, a fear of coming back, and the possible lack of interest in the online worship. One thing he mentioned is how being a new pastor meant that his personal styles and the way he runs the church has not really been established pre-pandemic. This means that, unlike tenured pastors, he pretty much only knows from this moment how ministry should be done. He mentioned how God has shown him how much of a blessing it is to be new, and how hard it would be to break 20+ years of ministry norms and tendencies in this time period. He stated it has most definitely had major effects on pastors so far, both positive and negative. For him, it has created a greater appreciation for the body of Christ. It has given him a new passion for preaching and teaching the Gospel. It has also challenged him to consider ministry under persecution should he face it in his lifetime.

Congregational Response

Member "Greta" Interview

When interviewing Greta, I set up a telephone call appointment by text. I promptly called her at our scheduled time; she picked up, and I introduced myself. We had a brief discussion about the study and how we are looking into the way the pandemic has impacted churches. Greta did not attend many online services because she helped with "Freewill Baptist's" online worship. The only online services she had seen were a couple on Wednesdays when she missed the in-person service. She mentioned that one of her concerns in the beginning of the pandemic was the potential for low attendance long-term. She said her brother-in-law, who suffers from mental illness, would not attend face-to-face services until everyone wore masks and practiced social distancing.

During the conversation, she discussed how the pandemic was a way God is trying to reach Christians to repent and do his will, and her opinion of God has not waivered. She knew of several friends on destructive paths, who had returned to church because of the pandemic. For example, she had a friend whose family would not allow her to leave the house. They have since changed and allow her to leave, but the mother became severely depressed during her time being homebound and is improving slowly. She was not able to hear the online service, so she had no connection to church. She wears a mask, gets out, and attends church in-person.

We talked about how the pandemic will affect the church in the future and how she felt the pastor handled it. The discussion had an overall positive feel, and she said the church might experience slower growth compared to before. The church and pastor had been doing a lot in the community with success before COVID, including things the pastor was helping to lead in the community. However, Greta was sure it would get back to pre-Covid levels over time. She really missed the InReach worship group meetings at member houses. OutReach has been a challenge because people do not answer their phones or doors, but she knows they will continue it when the pandemic is over. She was very complimentary of the pastor and the transition to online worship. While discussing the church's outreach ministries, she emphasized how awesome the pastor had been; meanwhile she has transitioned to doing everything she did prior to the pandemic by only adding wearing a mask. She emphasized how she wished everyone would have her same sentiment towards the pandemic and feels like the news media is horrible. She thinks they are not telling the whole truth about everything, feels terrible for people who think it is the end of the world, and if it is the end, then it is part of Gods plan.

Member "Tristen" Interview

I then reached out to Tristen, who was a little tougher to contact. After three text messages and two phone calls, I was finally able to reach him. We talked about how he was helping contribute to my study on the effects of the pandemic on the church. Tristen was active in the church before and during the pandemic as a deacon and volunteer. He was involved with video recording the current online worship services being posted on Facebook live, was the audio recorder for worship services posted on the churches YouTube ministry site since 2018, and has watched other church's online services, like John MacArthur and Jon Courson for years. He was not worried about how the pandemic would impact the church, and said attendance was about the same today since physical church started back. He missed the interaction with people from before the period when the church was online-only, though he felt like the core group of people helping with the online service had attended consistently throughout.

After the discussion about online and in-person church, we then explored his theology of the pandemic, what role God played, and how his pastor navigated the church during these turbulent times. First, he felt the virus was not a concern for him because of the time he spent as a police officer. He has had to adapt to the reality that when it is his time to go, he will join God in heaven. His views of God have remained consistent, and while God is sovereign and might not have caused it, God would find a way to use the pandemic for good. One way he sees God using the pandemic is in how it has expanded many people's use of internet services, especially the upcoming generation who is internet savvy and may better experience God online. A way he sees the pandemic as being bad for the future of church in general is the sheer number of people who have died because of the virus, and the second wave could prove to be more fatal. Aside from his apprehension of a second wave, Tristen was very impressed with the way the pastor has navigated their church through the pandemic so far. He complimented how he played the guitar and sang during the services, brought the church's online worship together, and how he communicated with everyone. He attributed the pastor's ability to adapt to the changes to his youthfulness.

Reflections & *Missio Dei*

My initial reflection on this study goes immediately to the pastor and how gracious he was with his personal time. He responded to texts or emails quickly and sincerely wanted to help in any way possible. This was my second project with "Kevin" involving a Pastor interview. I would like to say I am personally very thankful for these interactions. We differed on a few theological positions concerning hermeneutics and the pandemic, but we always found respectful ways to communicate through these differences. We found ways to center each other on Jesus and express our love for one another, even when we remained at odds. This time spent studying the pandemic together helped renew my belief that it is possible for God's different denominations to find common themes, lay differences aside, and put the Kingdom of God first.

I witnessed first-hand how a pastor who loves Jesus, and his congregation, should put personal opinions to the side and respect the choices of others, even when it may differ from his own. I learned how important it is that we trust in God's plan and still take thoughtful safety precautions. The study revealed how complicated issues, specifically stemming from a pandemic, are really opportunities for us to adapt and find hope, even when the walls felt like they were caving in. I observed how we are hardwired to be together physically as a community and separation impacts everyone in some way, shape, or form. It is obvious there is no challenge big enough to quell God's *Missio Dei*: not an earthquake, not a tidal wave, not a hurricane, not a tornado, not persecution, not racism, not sexism, not politics, not war, not hate, and especially not a pandemic!

Case Study Ten:
Lean on God as the Source of all Wisdom

Lea Gauthier

Lea Gauthier is both a doer and a learner of life, seeking to learn how to more fully lean on Jesus as she pursues Him and His purpose in her life. She is a wife, step-mom, sister, daughter, IT professional, and non-profit leader, currently relishing a season of study, as she pursues a depth of Biblical understanding through the MA Biblical Studies program at Asbury Theological Seminary.

Context: Suburban Ohio
Affiliation: Church of the Nazarene
Size: About 280 in attendance

Church Context

Congregations throughout the world responded to the Covid-19 pandemic of 2020 in a variety of ways. The following is just one example of how a Nazarene congregation located in suburban Ohio responded. The congregation is located on the outskirts of a major metropolitan city that was significantly impacted by the Covid-19 pandemic. It is of moderate size, reporting a membership of 426 members on their annual report as of June 1st, 2020. The lead pastor, Pastor David, reports that weekly attendance was approximately 280 individuals per week prior to the pandemic. Before the pandemic, the congregation held two Sunday morning worship services each week. Both services were of the same format, with a contemporary worship style. Services shifted to a single, online only service format in March 2020. Adult in-person Sunday morning services restarted at the end of May, with the children's Sunday morning program reopening in July. Small group and mid-week programing either stopped or shifted to a virtual meeting format in

March, and then gradually either restarted meeting in person within the suggested guidelines or remained remote at varying rates, based on the individual leaders and participants.

As part of the restart of in-person gatherings, adjustments were made to facilitate health guidelines. These included the removal of offering plates, mask wearing as a requirement for adult attendees, and modification to the check-in process for children to include the taking of temperatures. Chairs were rearranged in the sanctuary to provide for a six-foot spacing between families and hand shaking was discouraged. Two congregation members were interviewed, and both indicated a great deal of respect for the pastor and leadership team, and the decisions made. Neither felt the need to view other services during the pandemic and both returned to in-person services as soon as they were available. The overall theology of this congregation remained consistent prior to the pandemic and throughout. The pastor lives the ministry and theological practices that he teaches in his leadership of the congregation. His teaching and the ministry of this congregation illuminate the *Missio Dei*, God's Mission, in several ways.

Church Response & Social Media

The congregation leveraged social media heavily during the pandemic. Facebook was used prior to the pandemic, but the usage increased significantly, and very quickly ramped up in April. Prior to March, there were videos of both Sunday morning worship services and general announcements. The videos that appeared prior to March 2020 seemed to be an afterthought. Any electronic content, such as videos or presentation materials were not included in the Facebook video. Screens are visible in the sanctuary; however, they are primarily off screen for the video, so any displayed information is cut off and barely visible. Lighting is not optimal, and the speakers do not address the camera. Watching these videos leaves one with the impression that they are sneaking a peek of the service from the balcony and not really participating.

This all shifts quickly and dramatically in March. Beginning with March 12, 2020 Pastor David begins to use Facebook as a communication mechanism for the congregation to address the pandemic. In his first pandemic-oriented post he offers reassurances with scripture. Isaiah

41:10: "So do not fear, for I am with you; do not be dismayed, for I am your God. I will strengthen you and help you; I will uphold you with my righteous right hand". He then encourages the congregation and provides logistical details, both about the various service gatherings and what will be done to ensure the health and safety of the congregational members. A very early post in mid-March encourages community members who are elderly and in need of assistance with picking up groceries, or those in need of childcare to contact the church office. There are then posts, signed primarily by the lead pastor almost daily throughout the last two weeks of March. These posts are both encouraging and practical. He typically opens with scripture, provides a brief encouraging message, then launches into logistical details.

The Sunday morning services shift to an online only format, effective March 21, 2020. At this time, both times of worship are consolidated to a single time: 10:30 am. There is a dramatic shift over the next several services in both the technology and format of the online service and the pastor's comfort with preaching to an online audience. There is dramatic improvement in format, camera angle and lighting changes to make for a better experience. Electronic media, such as videos and slides are made available in the Facebook video. There is also a noticeable shift in Pastor David's delivery. He speaks to the camera and frequently acknowledges and engages with the online audience. He encourages watchers to use the comment section on Facebook, sing along with the worship music, open their bible and read along. He also encourages interactive participation by assigning "homework", giving suggestions for things people can do from home this week as well as suggested readings. In later sermons, he then makes references to these readings in a way that anticipates that the watcher has done them, however, such that if the viewer did not, the message could still be followed.

In addition to the live streamed Sunday Services, there are other areas that social media usage increased. There was a Wednesday evening time of prayer broadcast live for several weeks, as well as a "Faith Fridays" with various staff members. Other electronic platforms for remote meetings are used for small group bible studies such as Zoom. The platforms utilized are tailored to the audience, with the mention of Instagram as part of the Student Ministry. The direct usage of technology for connecting with the congregation is one that sees rapid transformation during the four-week period reviewed. In the weeks that follow, not only is there a drastic shift in technology that fully engages the remote audience, but the delivery by the pastor, as well as content, also engages with the remote audience. It is apparent in the beginning that the pastor is most comfortable interacting with a physically present audience, but as the weeks progress his comfort level with a virtual audience becomes apparent. The virtual attendee moves from a spectator hiding in the corner of the balcony to a fully engaged participant in the front seat conversing and engaging with Pastor David, if they so choose. There is an intentionality to worship that is refined during the Covid-19 pandemic.

Pastor David reminds his congregation that the church is not tied to a building; rather, the people are the Church. He refers to congregation as "the Church scattered" in the benediction. Each week, Pastor David encourages those watching from home to fully engage with the service. He encourages everyone to sing from home and to really make worship a time of togetherness, reminding his congregation that this does not need to be a religious broadcast. Even though the members of his congregation cannot be together in person, they can still worship together. There is an expectation that individuals will be engaging in the Word of God outside of scheduled times together. This emphasizes that life with Christ is not a weekly event that occurs in a building, but one that is seen through all aspects of life.

Easter services were one of the earliest online only service offerings. During Holy Week, there was a special Good Friday service on April 10, 2020. On Easter Sunday, April 12, 2020, there was a short, informal, sunrise video. It appears to have been taken from a phone and is in an outdoor residential setting. Pastor David plays guitar and sings, then offers a brief message on the hope found in the resurrection of Jesus.

During the main Sunday worship service on April 12, the primary focus is on the hope of Jesus, as seen in the resurrection. The service opens with a video reenactment of the resurrection and Mary's reaction. This service is focused on the resurrection of Jesus, as seen in the celebration of Easter. There is a message of Hope in that Jesus' death on Good Friday was not the last thing. The worst thing is not the last thing. Pastor David draws on the pandemic as an example of when we are feeling broken, as many are experiencing through the pandemic, Jesus can carry us through. Mary was a broken individual, yet Jesus used her. The pandemic is used as just one point of illustrating that the message God has for us is one of Hope. This is especially apparent in the resurrection of Jesus celebrated at Easter. The Easter resurrection message offered during this service is focused on Jesus, with minimal attention to the pandemic. The pandemic is a part of the present state, but it will not be the final state, and is not significant enough to consume the entire focus of this important message.

On April 19, 2020 Pastor David begins a series on Wisdom, focused on Proverbs. There is nothing about the sermon that indicates that it was chosen because of the current pandemic situation. However, Pastor David does occasionally draw on current events to illustrate a point. The primary theme of this week's message is that of Wisdom. He alludes to the need for wisdom in our world. He differentiates between knowledge and wisdom, characterizing wisdom as associated with application and doing. Wisdom ties actions to consequences. The wisdom literature, Proverbs specifically, provides guidelines. He encourages the seeking of wisdom through relationship with mentors. The message is tied to the pandemic by offering up practical suggestions for how relationships with mentors and discipling practices can continue in a time of social distancing. He addresses the pandemic by referring to the hardships that are being experienced during this time. He alludes to hardships that are secondary fall outs of the Covid-19 pandemic, such as economic hardship from job loss, and mental health impact from isolation, including depression and anxiety. Hardships provide an opportunity to gain wisdom if we learn from them. He reminds the congregation that longing to be with one another can be equated to and reminds us of our longing to be with God. We are not in charge of what happens to us, but we are in charge of how we respond to things that happen to us. This ties neatly back to how wisdom is how we act upon our knowledge and the consequences of our actions.

The message on April 26, 2020 continues the series on Wisdom. The primary theme of this message is the process for obtaining wisdom. This is done through listening and is a slow process. Pastor David emphasizes Jesus as the source of wisdom. There is also a role of community and shared testimony in obtaining wisdom. Once again, there is not a lot of focus on the pandemic in this message. Pastor David makes just a few references as illustrations. The pandemic provides us with an opportunity to learn patience as we struggle against the limitations it imposes on us. We should settle in and lean into God during this time. There are many opinions on what should be done, as, in America, we trust in our own opinion instead of God's. The pandemic can provide us with an opportunity to learn to trust in Him instead of earthly things. The communal story is a way to listen to one another to gain wisdom. Pastor David sees the pandemic has providing us with the opportunity to rediscover what our communal story is. During his time of prayer with and for the congregation, Pastor David reminds us that we should be grateful to be able to worship together online during this time. He prays for the leadership of those managing the pandemic and those experiencing job loss and financial hardship. He also addresses the mental health effects of the pandemic, in addition to the importance of showing honor and respect for those we disagree with.

May 3, 2020 is the final message in the Wisdom focused sermon series. In this service, he addresses wisdom, as exemplified through service or giving to others. Our own wisdom can be best observed by looking into the lives of those we serve. He continues with the comparison of wisdom versus knowledge. In this message, he compares knowledge to the education it may take to get a new job. He equates wisdom to how one may behave if that company then goes under due to unforeseen circumstance. The economic realities brought on by the pandemic bring direct practical application to this scenario. It is one's behavior in this type of situation that shows if they have wisdom to navigate. Their job-based knowledge will do them no good if the company is forced to close. It is their actions during this hypothetical crisis that illustrate either their wisdom or lack thereof. Wisdom is largely seen in how they treat others. He also draws on the pandemic to provide examples for how we should not use the current situation to prevent us from serving others and goes on to give very specific examples of how others can be served in a way that is within with the constraints of the pandemic.

Pastoral Approach

During the early days and weeks of the pandemic, Pastor David has approached his ministry to the congregation he serves with wisdom and a dynamic approach, both teaching and serving in a way that illustrates his own theology. He appears to have not been so caught up in the pandemic as his only focus, but rather has used the pandemic as a teaching tool when appropriate, and accommodated the logistics for both teaching and serving in a way that is consistent with what he teaches. There is an emphasis that the Church of Jesus Christ is not tied to a physical building, and that, while we long to be physically together, a spiritual togetherness is not dependent on a physical one. Pastor David acknowledges that there are many hardships introduced by the pandemic. Thus, he does not make light of them and seeks to acknowledge the wide spectrum of impacts from the pandemic. He offers the same general advice for all trials: lean into God, seeking wisdom from Jesus. He acknowledges that with the pandemic has come a wide array of emotional challenges, indicating that there may be those in the congregation who are experiencing depression, fear, and anxiety. He does not dismiss these but rather encourages the congregation to lean into Jesus during these challenging times.

The pandemic has forced an intentionality to worshiping God. The physical disconnect from the building is a reminder that the people are the church, the church is not the building. The pandemic has emphasized this truth. In the early days of the pandemic, Pastor David focused on the topic of Wisdom. He demonstrates wisdom through his own actions with leading his congregation. In teaching how to respond to the pandemic directly, there is an attitude of listening. He was not quick to teach a meaning to the pandemic, but, rather, focuses on how one should respond to it. His response is one of service. He both teaches on the importance of service and gives practical examples, and then also demonstrates them in his actions with leading the congregation in creative ways to serve others in the community. The congregation supports one another and their community with creative flexibility to work within the confines of social distancing stipulations. Pastor David appears to navigate a delicate balance between abiding by government regulations and guidance and placing trust and authority in God. He demonstrates respect for the authority of government leadership, advocating that his congregation members abide by the regulations for mask wearing and social distancing and offers up prayers for wisdom in their leadership. He looks to the guidance of medical professionals in making decisions around in person services and logistics for facilitating. He equates the wearing of a mask with demonstration of neighborly love. He also advises that one should not lean solely on the government for leadership, but that final authority rests with God. He states that Jesus in on the throne and will reign forever. This is a reminder to not only look to Jesus as our Lord, but also as our protector and comforter. In this way, Pastor David challenged his congregation members to not look to earthly things for reassurance, but to look heavenward. He demonstrates adaptability and flexibility, while also reminding his congregation of God's unwavering and unchanging love. He states very clearly that "Coronavirus is not his plan to take us down," and issues an invitation to lean into God during crisis and uncertainty.

The effects on his ministry appear to be relatively minimal once one overlooks the logistical challenges. Pastor David mentions that the biggest impact has been on the mechanism through which he ministers to others, indicating that he spends much more time on the phone now, praying with congregation members and offering pastoral care over the phone instead of in person. The biggest impact on his personal ministry is with hospital visits. Pastor David indicated that prior to the pandemic he would frequently spend time at the hospital, offering prayer and pastoral support. The visitor restrictions imposed make these visits impossible during the pandemic. This appears to be one key area of his ministry that does not accommodate an alternative that is within the health guidelines imposed. Other areas of ministry with healthy individuals appear to be supported and shifted to practices that are within the confines of the social distancing guidelines imposed by the pandemic.

Congregational Response

Pastor David and one of the congregation members indicated that a small number of regular attendees have chosen to leave the congregation, as they disagreed with the Pastor's stance on requiring members to wear masks to in-person services. The Pastor was not fazed by this choice and indicated that the number that made this decision was very small. Otherwise, neither the Pastor nor the congregation members indicated that they felt there would be any long-term detrimental impacts to their congregation. One member suggested that some of the minor changes during the in-person services, like logistics for the offering plate etc. were preferred and was hopeful that the changes would persist after the pandemic. Another member indicated that they were encouraged by the flexibility. Pastor David indicated willingness to continue with flexibility of engagement, suggesting that online engagement with the congregation was viable means of interacting with his congregation in the future. The Pastor did indicate that there were some members that were still choosing to not attend in-person services, despite participating in other in person activities in the community. This is another way that perhaps intentionality of worship has been refined during the pandemic.

This congregation appeared to weather the challenges of the pandemic without significant impact. Financial data was not available to indicate if there was a drop in tithing during the online only services; however, the Pastor did mention that the congregation was able to offer some financial aid during the crisis to families in need, both in the congregation and community, indicating that the Pastor did not have a financial or budgetary concern as part of the pandemic impact. There are some ministries, such as visiting those who are in hospitals that were particularly challenging to provide alternative accommodations for. However, in nearly every other area this congregation showed how with creativity there are still ways to serve and worship together in Christ within physical limitations.

Reflections & the *Missio Dei*

The Covid-19 pandemic has illustrated and brought several themes of the *Missio Dei* to the forefront of how this church seeks to understand its own mission. There was an immediate obvious reminder that the church is itself not a building. The mandatory physical removal of the congregational building from church services provided a stark reminder of the role it played. The ability of the congregation to navigate the peak of the pandemic restrictions without a physical building, or the ability to meet physically, illustrates how non-essential, yet highly desirable, it is. It emphasized the longing we may have for one another and how wonderful it is to have a physical space to worship together in. This can remind us of the longing we feel for Christ when we are separated from him. It has also served to reinforce how meaningful physical touch and contact is. While some activities and interactions can be conducted via electronic or virtual means, there are some things, such as physical presence at a hospital bedside that there is no replacement for. Removing and limiting these activities has reinforced how valuable they are.

The trials imposed by the pandemic have served as a refinement process. These trials have helped strip away the earthly material things that we may have focused on before, and in some instances brought to light the underlying attitudes and beliefs. When services shifted to online, it brought the worship of God into homes and required a different level of intentionality. In American culture there is a segregation of church life from home life from work life. Many can compartmentalize their different aspects of life because of the physical location of each. The physical separation and proximity to different people in each location, allows for a compartmentalization and different attitudes and behaviors in each setting. During the pandemic, there was a forcible collapse of all three of these structures into one physical location. If someone wanted to worship God, they had no choice but to invite God into their home. The availability of online live video viewing made this easy logistically, but required a different level of intentionality than attending a physical service. A physical service offers more than just worshiping God. It also provides an opportunity to experience worship music, interact with friends, and offers a degree of comfort and enjoyment with the presences of others in a special building dedicated to worship. Eliminating some of these enticements, such as the interaction with friends, makes an online worship experience more focused on God. There is also a level of temptation introduced with the ability to just "watch" it later. It becomes a very conscientious choice by each individual to either actively engage or simply spectate. The *Missio Dei* means incorporating and living out God's Word in every aspect of life. There is no room for compartmentalization of worship. Worship needs to occur in our homes and in our daily lives.

The *Missio Dei* involves engagement with God and the community. The pandemic has illustrated how engagement can occur both with Him and within our community in unique and creative ways, which we may have never fully appreciated, if not for the pandemic. It taught us that engagement is deeper than physical presence. One can be physically present and disengaged. Alternatively, if there is an intentionality to engagement, physical presence while very much appreciated, is perhaps not as critical as we may have previously thought. If one is intentional about it, connections can be made virtually and remotely. The necessity has shown how much easier it is with physical presence. God's mission is also relational. This congregation demonstrated that physical limitations were not going to be limiting in their relational aspects. They were creative with the use of outdoor space, chalk messages written on driveways, and window visits as examples of how physical distancing does not have to mean relational distance or lack of support for one another.

In reviewing the Facebook page and website for this Nazarene church, it is apparent that while they are not large enough to support their own dedicated social ministry, they actively engage in and support the social ministries of several organizations in their immediate vicinity. This includes civic activities within their local city context. Congregation members are encouraged to volunteer for city sponsored events. One of the very first Facebook posts related to the pandemic is an offer of assistance to the community for meeting immediate needs. Throughout the pandemic, they make it known that they are willing to help serve the needs of the community and their congregation members, in ways that are adapted to be within the pandemic health and safety parameters advised by the local government. They exemplify that, with a little creativity, physical restrictions do not prevent us from being the hands and feet of Christ to serve one another. They were able to serve one another and their community through prayer, yard work, running errands, financial support, and the man power support for other partnering organizations.

The final area of *Missio Dei* that this congregation exemplified was the prioritization of prayer. They both encouraged individual prayer and demonstrated that the act of corporate prayer did not require physical presence and proximity. This can be seen in the weekly Wednesday night dedicated times of prayer together online. Pastor David included prayers for the leadership navigating the challenges of the pandemic and those impacted by it during each Sunday service.

This congregation appears to have done an excellent job pulling together and continuing to grow together and minister to their community. The Covid-19 pandemic has, in many ways, served as a refinement fire for this American church. Those individuals who were lukewarm in their faith and allowed the lack of a weekly Sunday in person service to create separation between themselves and God likely did not have a true relationship and have been burned away. Congregations who relied solely on a large in person Sunday time of gathering may not have had the strength of relationships to hold their congregation together.

Placing the American Church in the fire has driven several issues to the surface. The issue of mask wearing has taken such a political tone that it has driven members of this congregation away. In this suburban Ohio area, there is a large non-denominational mega church that refused to cancel in person services and advocates that abiding by government regulations demonstrates fear. They proclaim a message that faith over fear and Jesus' power over Covid-19 as an excuse to not abide by the government guidance. This has created an overwhelmingly poor Christian witness in the wider community. In this region, there are two conflicting messages around mask wearing that has unfortunately created divisiveness amongst the Christian community. One theology that is advocated by the Nazarene church is that mask wearing demonstrates neighborly love. The other, opposing view, as held by the non-denominational mega church, advocates that mask wearing demonstrates fear and lack of trust in God. This issue demonstrates the poor outcome that arises with the mixing of political agenda with Christian witness. The other theological issue that has arisen is the idea of trust in Jesus balanced against respect for governmental authorities. There is a difference in respecting the authority of an earthly leadership while still placing one's ultimate trust and faith in the heavenly Kingdom. This can be a challenging line to walk and requires wisdom, not just knowledge, to navigate.

Another important aspect of the *Missio Dei* is the need to listen. To effectively minister to the global community, we need to listen to others, to learn their culture and needs. We need to be filled with humility to understand how to best serve without jumping to conclusions and false teaching. This idea of the need to listen is just as relevant when it comes to ministering to our immediate community during a time of crisis. The Covid-19 pandemic has illuminated the importance of listening to gain wisdom and differentiating between action based on knowledge versus wise choices. It has also elevated the importance of neighborly love. When we put others first and err on the side of love, then while we cannot be guaranteed we will always make the correct choices with these difficult decisions, but we will have a more likely chance of doing the right thing. Taking a stance that errs on the side of loving others always leads to a better witness.

The Covid-19 pandemic has shattered some of our expectations about what is required to be a church community and illuminated what is most important. We long for what we did not fully appreciate before with the freedom to be fully physically together in a way that we long for Christ. Just as we were only able to be superficially with one another during the pandemic, we are only superficially able to be with Christ. The depth of our connection with one another, and with Christ, is driven by the intentionality of our choice to engage. We have learned that while physical presence in a building is not required to be the church, it is wonderful to be physically in one another's presence. Engagement and intentionality of worship is not restricted to physical presence. One can be in a church building and disengaged, or at home and fully engaged. Imagine however how wonderful it will be when we can be fully physically present in intentional worship with Him?

Technology can be used as an amazing tool to connect us to one another when we leverage it appropriately. However, I think we do need to use caution about creating too much of an individualized and consumeristic approach to ministry. A Sunday morning worship service is not a spectator event to be viewed from a distance, but one to be engaged in with intentionality and purpose. This pandemic may have created an opportunity for those who were not fully engaged to disengage further. Rather than creating a new divide, I think it just emphasized an emotional divide that was likely already present, but not visible. With a newly renewed and refined Church, the body of Christ will come out of this pandemic stronger, with more focus and intentionality. I do not doubt that it will look different, but the American church is in desperate need of a revolutionary change Perhaps this is just the beginning that change.

The intentionality of each of our choices has been amplified during the Covid-19 pandemic. To wear a mask or not is a choice that makes a statement to everyone you encounter. Where to go, and who to spend time with, has taken on a level of intentionality and choice. C.S. Lewis articulates the choices before us and the ramifications of those choices in the book The Great Divorce.

> "There are only two kinds of people in the end: those who say to God, "Thy will be done," and those to whom God says, in the end, "Thy will be done." All that are in Hell, choose it. Without that self-choice there could be no Hell. No soul that seriously and constantly desires joy will ever miss it. Those who seek find. Those who knock it is opened." – C.S. Lewis, The Great Divorce

The Covid-19 Pandemic has changed the American Church because of the choices that each of us have and will continue to make. The question always was and will be, what choice will we make?

Case Study Eleven: God has a Greater Purpose Behind the Suffering

Bryce Holdman

Bryce Holdman is the pastor at Mt. Horeb United Methodist Church in Lexington, SC, and is a first-year student at Asbury Theological Seminary, with a goal of pursuing church planting and pastoring in the future.

Context: Suburban Florida
Affiliation: Church of God (Pentecostal)
Size: About 200 members

Introduction

For the sake of this assignment, I chose to study a congregation located in a smaller city in Florida. My uncle is actually the pastor of this congregation, and has been for a number of years now. I intend to refer to this church as New Sound Church, though this is not the church's actual name. Throughout this congregational study, I have learned much about the church's response to the COVID-19 pandemic, not only within the city, but also across America. There have been numerous learning curves directly from this study that I have sought to apply to my own ministry context, many of which will be highlighted in the examination of findings below. God is on the move through the congregation of New Sound Church, and I believe that the *Missio Dei* can be clearly seen through their ministry.

Church Context

To begin our analysis of this study, I would like to first give some overview information regarding the congregation of New Sound Church. The denominational affiliation of the church is under the umbrella of the Church of God, a branch of Pentecostalism. The pastor of this church has a background in the Church of God denomination, obtaining multiple degrees from COG institutions, along with growing up in the COG himself. When it comes to membership, New Sound has around 200 members. Their regular attendance tends to supersede this number by about 40-50 (pre-COVID). However, during their season of online ministry, the pastor of this church noted that their numbers had actually progressively decreased based on virtual views. He also was sure to note that he personally believes that they will see an increase in attendees post COVID, with the catalyst being a new building that will be built within the next 2 years, Lord willing.

This church finds itself located in South Florida, which is considered a suburban area near both Miami and Fort Myers. The population in this area fluctuates but is normally just under 20,000 residents. With this fluctuation in residency during different seasons of the year, New Sound Church experiences a spike in attendance during the winter months. In terms of the COVID-19 impact in this area, I found that the city has seen slightly less impact than other parts of Florida. Their beaches are currently reopened and thriving. Much of this is due to snowbirds (those who come for the winter season only). Many of these travelers have been delaying their arrival due to COVID, which has allowed the city to have significantly less people than normal around this time of year.

Church Response & Social Media

Moving back to the church itself, one can experience a blend of contemporary and traditional worship styles. While watching the different services in April and May from New Sound, I found that many of the worship songs chosen were contemporary songs, performed in a traditional manner. Much of the worship was filmed in a house, with 3 vocalists sitting around a piano, often played by the pastor himself. This seemed to be a consistent trend throughout the videos produced during the season of online-only ministry. Speaking of consistency, the pastor made sure to let me know that he intended to find specific ways to be consistent throughout their season of online videos. Worship was one of many ways he achieved this, another being the same format for each sermon.

When watching the four services throughout April and May, I noticed that the video quality was high. However, the animation that was included in each of these videos was poor. Much of this issue was due to a lack of resources when it comes to production quality. Nonetheless, the pastor sought to find consistency during these sermons through the location in which they were filmed. Each sermon was recorded in the main auditorium on the stage, with the pastor seated on a stool by himself. He clearly knew his content extremely well, as he rarely looked at any notes he had with him, focusing mainly on the audience behind the camera. Due to this tactic, the sermons felt very personal and relatable from the very start of each message.

The first service viewed was New Sound's Easter worship service on April 12th. This video, along with every other, was prerecorded and released on the following Sunday. This video, in particular, included primarily contemporary music, with three vocalists around a piano singing three songs. From here, the video switched to the auditorium, where the pastor began his message. The sermon was entitled "Reassurance of a Living Hope", referencing 1 Peter 1:3-7 and Romans 12:12 as the main Scripture passages. He also referenced the COVID pandemic in a unique way, talking about Jesus' agony when going to the cross. Jesus did this because He knew the Father had a greater purpose behind the agony and pain. The pastor went on to relate this to the pandemic, noting God's higher purposes behind it. Paired with this, the pastor believes that this pandemic is some sort of dress rehearsal for what life could be like post-normal. In response to the pastor's message, he desires that his congregation experience the hope inside of them that tells them they will make it through. At this point, the regulations responding to the pandemic had only been in effect for about one month. Interestingly, at the close of this Easter service, there were two individuals that performed interpretive dancing to the song, "The Blessing". Though this was a unique touch, I was confused as to how it tied into the rest of the service.

Nonetheless, the Easter message seemed to lay the foundation for the following messages to come from the pastor in the next few weeks. On April 19th, New Sound's video once again opened with a time of worship around a piano. One of the songs chosen was the popular contemporary worship song, "Waymaker". This song highlights the truth about God that He does indeed make a way when it seems like there's no way, relating well to the pandemic situation going on at the time. When it came time for the sermon, the pastor titled his message "Resetting our Priorities". Matthew 6:33 was used as the main Scriptural reference, culminating in the pastor declaring that God is still in control. He encourages his congregation to remain faithful, believing this truth, knowing that God is using this pandemic somehow. There was yet another creative element in this video, between the time of worship and sermon. There was a testimony given from a young congregation member of what life has been like in the pandemic. This was most likely a strategic move on the pastor's behalf, using this testimony as a connection point to make this video feel as personal to those at home as possible. The concept of making these videos as personal as possible trickled down to the April 26th video as well, when the pastor threw in numerous personal stories throughout his message.

His sermon was about having stronger faith, citing 2 Corinthians 13:5-9 as the main text. This time around, prior to the sermon, the music selection was mainly traditional, singing a number of hymns that remind us of God's strength, once again around a piano. During his sermon, the pastor referenced the pandemic as something that God is using to grow and strengthen our faith. In response to this belief, the pastor desires that his congregation seek to see this season as an opportunity to renew their minds and strengthen their faith in Christ.

I concluded my study of New Sound's online worship services with their video from May 3rd. This time around, they began once again with contemporary worship, performed in a traditional type of way. After this, the pastor began his sermon, speaking about how to stay the course. He used Hebrews 12:1-3 as his main Scriptural reference, talking about the weariness that people are feeling in the pandemic. He challenged his congregation to stay the course and keep running the race. The way in which we do this, according to the pastor, is by staying close to the Word of God. As it relates to the pandemic, the pastor recognizes that the devil is in the business of trying to distract people from the joy to be experienced. However, any further references in the sermon to the pandemic were minimal.

Throughout his messages, the pastor seemed each week to mention the pandemic as the elephant in the room briefly, but did not choose to focus on it while preaching. This seemed to be a strategic, intentional tactic employed by the pastor, one that also trickled into the social media presence. In terms of social media, New Sound put all of their weekly videos on Vimeo, a platform similar to YouTube where users can upload videos. However, due to their current technological resources, New Sound was not able to livestream any of their services or online events. So, all videos were previously recorded. When it comes to social media platforms utilized throughout the week, I spent some time studying both their Facebook and Instagram pages.

First, on Instagram, New Sound has a total of 186 followers. This seems to align well with the total number of regular attendees that the church has. After looking at their following, it is important to see how often they are posting and what types of posts they most often employ. Studies show that in order to boost engagement on Instagram, the first step must be posting regularly, with different types of content. Most utilized are pictures taken from key events and services in person. These allow for followers to interact with a more personal post than a mere graphic. In saying that, New Sound also posts a good number of graphics relating to events they have coming up. For instance, around Christmas time, they began an initiative called "Buy a Tree, Change a Life". In order to promote this initiative, New Sound posted a graphic that explains the details. There are also a few short videos posted to the Instagram account, most of which are recordings from the Sunday morning time of worship.

After looking at their Instagram account from an overview perspective, I honed in on the timeframe when the church was functioning strictly online, due to the pandemic. What I found was that nearly all of their posts to Instagram were graphics. These posts got an average of 7 likes, compared to the images, which get an average of 15 likes. Much of the reason there were strictly graphics being posted during the season of quarantine was due to a lack of photo opportunities at church events.

However, I believe there should have been some videos posted during this time. Out of all types of posts one could make to Instagram, videos will naturally get the most engagement, which proves true even in the case of New Sound, as their videos all have an average of 90 views.

Facebook was similar in many ways, but had a few differences, as it relates to social media engagement. Rather than having 186 followers, as their Instagram account has, New Sound's Facebook page has a total of 964 likes, showing that this platform seems to be most utilized by them. Since being back in person for services, Facebook is where the church will post their Sunday morning videos. This allows people watching to chat live, as the church seems to have upgraded to a livestream option for their congregants still watching from home. There is a dedicated staff member who is answering questions and interacting with online viewers in the chat. Their most recent Sunday morning video on Facebook got just under 400 views, a significant increase from any posts or videos on both Instagram and Vimeo. Much of this is due to how many people spend time on Facebook compared to Instagram and Vimeo. The church's demographic are mainly families with older children. Many of these people spend hours on Facebook each week, interacting with friends of theirs, including their church family. New Sound has done a decent job of creating a sense of community online, mainly through Facebook it seems.

Pastoral Approach

Overall, all three of these platforms for social media are utilized week to week. Though Facebook is most commonly used for posting pictures and videos, Instagram is another outlet to reach many of their students and younger attendees. The pastor himself tells me that he has spent countless hours gathering information about social media, and putting together a strategy for their church. This seems to be paying off in many ways, especially since the pandemic began back in March. It has forced New Sound, and many other churches, to use more and more social media platforms to engage with their community. This leads me into a discussion about the pastor's approach to ministry during this pandemic.

One of the initial, key questions I sought to have answered when speaking to the pastor on the phone was the church's involvement in mission and serving opportunities amidst COVID-19. Their largest outlet for this was a partnership with Meals of Hope. Once a week, there would be deliveries through this organization to families, much of which was resourced by New Sound's people. Along with this involvement, the church essentially became a host site for "No Little Hungry Tummies Left Behind". This initiative gave out 400-500 fresh lunches prepared by a local restaurant every day for five days a week. The staff and congregation actively participated in this serving opportunity.

Paired with serving opportunities in the community, I asked the pastor how he sought to minister from afar during the lockdown. He told me that right away, he and his staff took the time to divide the church directory amongst five different families. Each of these families called the church attendees on their list every week to check in on them and offer prayer or assistance in any way they could. While speaking to the two congregation members I talked with, I learned that this was a meaningful and memorable experience for New Sound's people during the quarantine. There were also two major holidays celebrated in unique ways during the lockdown.

First, New Sound came up with an idea called "Easter in a Box". This was an interactive box, mainly for families with young children, to follow along during the Easter service posted to Vimeo. From what the pastor told me, this was a huge success. The second holiday was Mother's Day, when New Sound had a drive-thru for moms, giving out Bundt cakes as they came through. Outside of these holidays, once some restrictions were lifted, the church had fun events outdoors, like movie nights, which included many of the younger families in the congregation. All around, the pastor tells me that he and the staff did a good job of engaging with their community from afar.

The pastor also had to partake in two funerals during the pandemic. Both of these were Spanish-speaking funerals. Apparently, there was hardly any social distancing or mask wearing at these events. The pastor told me that this was mainly a cultural difference. Both of these, nonetheless, were meaningful times of celebration of life for the congregation members involved. This also gave them the opportunity to interact with their pastor in person. Overall, the pastor and his team did a phenomenal job engaging with their congregation members during the lockdown.

In light of the pandemic, I also got a chance to speak with the pastor about his theology, as it relates to COVID-19. Within this conversation, he told something that impacted me greatly: the Church is not ready for the harvest, rather than the harvest not being ready for the Church. The pastor told me a story about one night when he was out stargazing with his wife on their back porch during the lockdown. He was praying, asking God to show him a glimpse of what His higher purposes were behind all of this. The pastor feels that the Holy Spirit spoke to him in that moment the words recited above. He went on to tell me that he feels local churches in the west especially love their model more than their mission. I agree with this analysis. The church I currently serve at hosts around 5,000 members. More than half of these come to our contemporary worship services on a Sunday morning. These services are full of fancy lights, many cameras, and incredible music, all of which are used to enhance the worship experience. However, there is a temptation to focus more heavily on production elements than focusing on the message being given: the Gospel. It is a danger for local churches to fall in love with the idea of a large and exciting church. And in the process, the emphasis behind the local church will shift. The pastor of New Sound believes this is happening right now. This is true, especially in light of the greater shift to online ministry due to COVID-19, as there is the potential to prioritize the production over everything else. Thus, the local church will then become like Hollywood.

The pastor also has had a shift in his own life in terms of ministry. He has seen firsthand that the emotional needs of an individual are currently in the forefront of their minds, rather than on the back burner. There is much fear and uncertainty present inside of people. So, in response, the New Sound team has sought to focus more heavily on these things. A practical way this is done from afar is through sermon topics. The pastor strategically chose topics for sermons during the lockdown based upon what he felt his people needed to hear about, due to what they were struggling with at the time. This leads into a discussion about the effects the pandemic has had on the congregation itself.

One of the first things the pastor and I talked about was specifically how the season of lockdown affected the congregation. He noted that his analysis shows that people within his congregation enjoy having the option of watching online. One of my personal predictions on the other side of COVID-19 is that many church-goers will continue to watch from home, where it is most comfortable. It requires less effort, especially for those with young children. However, the pastor of New Sound made it clear that he does not feel any of his church attendees will continue to watch from home consistently once the pandemic is over or minimized. He sees this as an added option for those who are traveling out of town on the weekends occasionally, but also as an opportunity to extend the reach of his church. All this to say, the online option will be continuing past the pandemic, as it is an added resource to New Sound.

Surprisingly, the pastor went on to make clear that most of his congregation were holding up well emotionally and spiritually during the lockdown. Though the two congregants I spoke with told me about a feeling of isolation and loneliness they felt at certain points, they also highlighted the role of weekly phone calls in their overall emotional and spiritual health. And when the congregation had finally returned to in-person worship services, the pastor noted that the changes he noticed were minimal. He claimed that there was a sense of awkwardness when people were embracing one another, not knowing whether it was socially acceptable or not. Upon this point, the pastor also told me that he felt as if virtual connection (online) does a decent job facilitating, but not accommodating. There are many more potential bumps in the road with online community due to internet connections. Therefore, once his congregation was back in person, the pastor noticed great joy, knowing that even if it were socially distanced, the church family was back together.

When wrapping up my conversation with the pastor of New Sound, we had a brief discussion on the topic of potential long-term effects on both his individual congregation, as well as the global Church. He noted that in terms of his own congregation, he feels that growth will be slow, but it will indeed happen, both in person and online. Many people in the Naples area are more interested in a relationship with Christ, due to the frustration and uncertainty the pandemic has caused them. I personally believe this concept is a trend elsewhere as well. There are many in South Carolina, where I currently serve, that are beginning to ask questions about Christianity due to this season we have been in together. I saw a shift from people blaming COVID-19 on God initially, to now many people inviting Him to help them have joy in the midst of it.

Speaking from a more global perspective on the Church, the pastor believes that there will be a completely different look for the Church going forward. There has already been a "filtering out" of certain people that are too comfortable in their faith in local churches all across America, and may transcend globally. This comment alludes to my earlier prediction that many will choose to watch church from home far past the pandemic. The pastor told me that though this trend was not present within his own congregation, he has seen it first-hand all across America. These things were echoed by the two congregation members I spoke with from New Sound as well.

Congregational Response

After posing a similar question about the future of the Church to the two congregants, I heard very similar answers from them both. In essence, both believe that those whom are able to "stick it out" with the strength and encouragement of Christ will be alright. Though it may not look as we want it to, God's still in control. This was an encouragement to me, as I can see the great faith these two congregants had. One of them in particular referenced September 11th, 2001. They noted that on this day, no one woke up in America expecting our country to be different forever by the end of the day. When tragedy came upon us, seemingly out of nowhere, we initially responded with grief. Yet, even in our grief, we had a sense of greater unity. This congregation member believes that out of this pandemic will come a greater sense of unity within the Church. When those that don't yet have a faith in Christ see that unity, they will want to be a part of it.

Reflections & the *Missio Dei*

Overall, my conversations with both the pastor and two of the New Sound congregation members were very intriguing and influential. There were nuggets of wisdom that I personally received from all three of these conversations relating to local church ministry, especially in a global pandemic. Throughout my careful study of New Sound's response to COVID-19, I found that this church is a prime example of what it looks like to partake in the *Missio Dei*, even when circumstances shift. The main takeaways I have from this study can be defined and expounded upon as follows.

First, I have seen very clearly through this study that God is still able to cultivate community through a strictly online platform. Many churches like New Sound have decided to focus much attention and energy toward creating a more engaging online experience during worship on Sunday mornings. However, the pastor and his team at New Sound have done a fantastic job finding virtual touch points not just on Sunday mornings, but throughout the week. Phone calls made to congregation members each week was a very clear way to commune, paired with a sense of ownership when beginning initiatives such as the ones mentioned in this study, even during the lockdown. When people are able to participate in their faith with a community of believers, rather than simply observe others doing so, it grants them fulfillment from the Holy Spirit. This seems to be the goal of the pastor and his team at New Sound.

Second, as a pastor myself, this study has shown me the importance of turning an ear to your congregation, specifically in times of great need and uncertainty. The pastor of New Sound was able to be an incredible listener when it came to crafting his messages. As noted previously in this study, he spoke to specific needs that his people had during the pandemic. He showed the truth of Scripture amidst these needs, allowing God to comfort them through the power of the Holy Spirit. This, once again, gave the desired family feel to the congregation members, serving as a great example of Paul's words in Galatians 6:2, when he says, "Carry each other's burdens, and in this way you will fulfill the law of Christ".

Third, God is certainly using the pandemic in many ways. Some of these we can see. Others of these we cannot yet. Either way, in talking with the pastor and congregation members from New Sound, I can see that they are witnesses of how God is moving in the midst of this unprecedented time. Many of them had taken physical community for granted. However, this is now such a greater meaning behind getting to come together each week as a church family and body of believers. Their faith has been strengthened each week through powerful times of worship and inspiring messages from the pastor. This has allowed the congregation to come back in person with one another hungrier than ever before to increase their faith each week.

Finally, I was able to witness firsthand the extremely intentional commitment that New Sound Church has to the *Missio Dei*. The mission of God can be clearly witnessed in many verses throughout Scripture. For instance, in Habakkuk 2:14, the Lord says, "For as the waters fill the sea, the earth will be filled with an awareness of the glory of the Lord." References to God's mission like these, however, only tell us what the mission is. It is our job as the Church and body of Christ to choose willingly to participate in it with God. New Sound has done a fantastic job empowering their congregation to take ownership of their faith in this kind of way. This was mainly done through the outreach opportunities mentioned earlier in this examination of their ministry. They engaged well with the surrounding Naples area, even amidst COVID-19 restrictions.

The congregation at New Sound also seems to be very missional focused in its nature. The pastor made sure to let me know about a building expansion happening within the next two years or so, which will allow the church to accommodate for even more people in the Naples area on Sunday mornings. They are currently in the planning phase of how to launch this building campaign, as well as how to go about getting the community involved somehow. By my understanding, much of the mission of God has to do with finding a balance between a "come and see" and "go and tell" mindset in one's ministry.

The "come and see" portion is the part which many local churches thrive at week to week. They are able to create a phenomenal worship experience for their people, and those in the community will often naturally come and see what it is all about. This is a great evangelistic strategy, especially when one has many resources available to draw people in. However, there must also be a "go and tell" part of one's ministry.

The "go and tell" doesn't have to be overseas in some third-world country. Instead, I believe Jesus' desire is for us to tell those around us about the love of God. This can be done in many different ways, some of which New Sound displayed beautifully. From my conversations with the two congregation members I spoke with, I learned that many of the congregants at New Sound have a heart for getting friends in the community to this church on Sunday mornings. This goes beyond Sunday's in some cases, as many will take the initiative to invite people to fun events, like movie nights. This is another evangelistic opportunity that allows congregants to actively participate with God in His mission. But it requires obedience on our end.

Conclusively, my study of New Sound Church in South Florida was a successful endeavor. Through conversations with the pastor, as well as two key congregation members, I was able to learn about the thriving ministry going on within this church. I see the *Missio Dei* as extremely prevalent in the ministries happening around New Sound and have no doubt that the people of this congregation are actively participating in God's mission. I look forward to keeping up with how the ministry is going for New Sound down the road, especially in light of a brand-new building project coming up very soon. This is certainly an effective church in the Naples, Florida area. Even amidst the COVID-19 pandemic, this congregation led by this phenomenal pastor, is making an impact for the Kingdom of God in lives every day. I pray that it continues and only grows stronger.

Case Study Twelve: Hope is a Person, Named Jesus

Stephen M. Horst

Stephen Horst, a missionary under Eastern Mennonite Missions, has lived in Thailand since 2013, making disciples and developing leaders among the Isaan people group.

Context: Small-town Western Virginia
Affiliation: Mennonite
Size: 600 members

Introduction

When the first case of Coronavirus disease 2019 (COVID-19) appeared in the state of Virginia on March 7, "Public health officials caution[ed] that evidence [had] not been seen of COVID-19 spreading in Virginia and said the risk is low."[1] In little over a month, however, the small western Virginia city of Princetown[2] would find itself in the grip of a worldwide pandemic. On March 12, about one month before Holy Week, Virginia Governor, Ralph S. Northam would declare a state of emergency in response to the increasing spread of COVID-19.[3] Many were hopeful that after a couple of weeks, the number of new COVID-19

[1] Commonwealth of Virginia, Virginia Department of Health. "First Virginia Case of COVID-19 Confirmed at Fort Belvoir." Newsroom, 7 Mar. 2020, www.vdh.virginia.gov/news/2020-news-releases/first-virginia-case-ofcovid-19-confirmed-at-fort-belvoir/

[2] All names, including names of places, churches, and people have been changed to maintain anonymity.

[3] Northam, Ralph S. Executive Order Number Fifty-Five (2020): Temporary Stay at Home Order Due to Novel Coronavirus (COVID-19). Commonwealth of Virginia, Office of the Governor, 30 Mar. 2020, www.governor.virginia.gov/media/governorvirginiagov/executive-actions/EO-55-Temporary-Stay-at-Home-Order-Due-to-Novel-Coronavirus-(COVID-19).pdf. Accessed 4 Dec. 2020.

cases would peak, and life would resume as normal. However, it would not be until May 15 that restrictions, intended to stem the spread of infection, would begin to relax.[4] By then, outbreaks at meat processing plants and nursing homes would push the small city of Princetown to the top of Virginia's case count list, and COVID-19 would claim the lives of 21 residents.[5]

Church Context

Princetown Mennonite Church (PMC), is a congregation six-hundred members strong, located in the heart of the growing college town of Princetown. In a denomination based historically in countryside farming communities, PMC was the first Mennonite missional endeavor to establish a congregation in the city of Princetown. While still considered a "mission" of the denomination's regional district, PMC planted several other churches in the city before itself receiving the title of "church". Twice in the course of the church's history, in an effort not to become too large to maintain a sense of intimate community, upon reaching a membership of around 300, a significant portion of the congregation would launch another church plant within the city.

In time, PMC would begin to shift toward the formation of Sunday School classes instead of planting separate churches, growing into a comparatively large congregation by Mennonite standards. In this way, congregants would connect with a more intimate expression of church, growing together in discipleship, while participating in a larger congregation, drawing from the synergy of a larger body of believers. Today there are sixteen such Sunday School communities at PMC, established largely among generational lines, in which members study scripture, grow spiritually as disciples of Jesus, support one another in relationship, and explore God's personal and corporate call into the God's mission in the world – the *Missio Dei*. Members and staff often use

[4] Northam, Ralph S. "Executive Order Number Fifty-One (2020): Declaration of a State of Emergency Due to Novel Coronavirus (COVID-19)" Commonwealth of Virginia, Office of the Governor, 12 March 2020, www.governor.virginia.gov/media/governorvirginiagov/governor-of-virginia/pdf/eo/EO-51-Declaration-of-a-State-of-Emergency-Due-to-Novel-Coronavirus-(COVID-19).pdf. Accessed 17 Dec. 2020.

[5] Commonwealth of Virginia, Virginia Department of Health. "COVID-19 in Virginia: Locality." Coronavirus, Dec. 2020, www.vdh.virginia.gov/coronavirus/coronavirus/covid-19-in-virginia-locality/

the word "family" to describe PMC's Sunday School classes, highlighting the central role they play in congregational life. Each class has its own distinct name, culture, and rotating leadership structure sourced from within the group. This Sunday School program of PMC could accurately be called the "backbone" of the congregation.

PMC is mostly an affluent, aging white church in an increasingly diverse city. A hub for refugee resettlement, the city of Princetown is proud to have over fifty languages spoken in the homes of children in the local school system, despite a modest population of around 50,000 residents.[6] Recognizing the relative lack of ethnic and economic diversity in the congregation, and in an effort to build relationship and witness in the neighborhood surrounding the church building, PMC engages in various forms of outreach. One such outreach is in a nearby complex of apartments, focusing on children's programs, Vacation Bible Schools, and providing transportation to its Wednesday evening programming. This is reflected in the PMC vision statement, which affirms a call to community, worship, discipleship and friendship with the neighboring community.

The leadership structure of PMC is a three-way combination lay teams and paid staff. A ten-member church council establishes the congregation's priorities, stewards administration, and provides accountability for the staff. Nine paid staff, including Lead Pastor Larry, Associate Pastors Stephanie and Scott, and Music Director Jon, provide spiritual leadership within the congregation. A four-member team of elders seeks to provide discernment, guidance and encouragement.

Theologically, PMC identifies strongly with Anabaptism (from the Greek for 'rebaptizer'), a radical movement within the Protestant Reformation that gave birth to such expressions of the Church as the Mennonites, Amish and Quakers.[7] Distinguishing tenets include adult

---

[6] Taken from the Wikipedia article on the city of "Princetown" – not cited here to preserve anonymity.

[7] "Schleitheim Confession: Anabaptist Confession." Britannica, Encyclopaedia Britannica, edited by Matt Stefon, ed., www.britannica.com/topic/Schleitheim-Confession. Accessed 17 Dec. 2020.

believer's baptism, separation of church from the state, leadership by 'shepherds,' non-violence, and the refusal to swear oaths.[8]

Church Response & Social Media

As COVID-19 infections began to be confirmed in Virginia, Gov. Northam declared a state of emergency on March 12. Two days prior, on Tuesday, March 10, PMC staff had already begun to communicate with the congregation by email about initial changes in effect for the Sunday ahead. By this point, no cases had been confirmed in Princetown. However, by Friday, March 13, as the first local case was confirmed, and a nation-wide state of emergency was declared, more email communications went out. The first, sent around 10:00 AM, discouraged congregants over the age of sixty from gathering in Sunday School classes, or attending worship. They were encouraged to worship remotely via live stream or to tune in to an AM radio broadcast. By that evening, around 7:00 PM, following a declaration by Gov. Northam that schools would be closed for the next two weeks, Pastor Larry would send a second email saying that "all activities at [Princetown] Mennonite Church are cancelled for the next two weeks." On the decision to send that email, Pastor Larry would recount in an October 19 interview, "When the governor issued his mandates for businesses, churches and other gatherings, there was conversation involving all of the ministry staff, with church council chair and elders' chair. The decision was ultimately mine, as it fell under policy governance. [There were] multiple conversations. Getting the sense of what church council wanted for safety, operating by all the guidelines from the government, the elders concurred" that activities should be suspended.

On the first Sunday apart, March 15th, the PMC published its first podcast. With a patchwork system, using personal smart phones and existing equipment, PMC staff tried to make things work with the audio-only podcast. However, they ran into difficulty with the Streaming format, possibly due to the high level of internet traffic that Sunday. The following Sunday, they attempted to live-stream a video podcast. However, in Pastor Larry's words, "it felt like an utter failure. So, we shut that down and aimed at Easter. We did the [audio] podcast for another

[8] "Anabaptist: Protestantism." *Encyclopedia Britannica*, www.britannica.com/topic/Anabaptists.

couple of weeks, then switched over to weeks, then switched totally over to YouTube format for Easter."

By Easter Sunday, April 12, the staff were more ready to go live, having upgraded some of their equipment and training, though some technical glitches persisted. By the next Sunday, April 19, and onward, they abandoned live video podcast, in favor for an entirely prerecorded service. The staff would gather on Thursday mornings to record their parts, including calls to worship, the "talk" – a very pared down version of a sermon more suitable for shortened remote attention spans – followed by a question-and-answer discussion time, a pastoral prayer and a benediction. The finished video would be broadcast every Sunday morning (barring technical difficulties) for the congregation to join together remotely in worship at 10:00 AM. PMC made the choice early on to focus on a video worship experience that could be enjoyed equally by all, as long as members were needing to worship remotely due to the pandemic. In this way, all members, regardless of age, health, or need to quarantine, would be able to engage in worship in the same way.

April 12, 2020 – Easter Sunday

As Princetown's new cases reached an average of around 15 per 100,000 residents each day[9] (compared to the state-wide rate of 4.4[10] and nation-wide rate of 9.5[11]), PMC broadcast its first full service in video streaming in on YouTube. The "chat room" on the screen's side panel was lively, as the congregation exchanged greetings, words of encouragement and appreciation, and as volunteers gave each other pointers and suggestions, particularly for the audio mix. Pastors Larry and Scott, seated six feet apart in a "living room" setting in the church lobby, with a cozy fireplace centrally framed, worked hard to bridge the gap between them and the congregants, watching from their homes. Using

---

[9] Commonwealth of Virginia, Virginia Department of Health. "COVID-19 in Virginia: Locality." Coronavirus, Dec. 2020, www.vdh.virginia.gov/coronavirus/key-measures/pandemic-metrics/locality-metrics/

[10] Commonwealth of Virginia, Virginia Department of Health. "COVID-19 in Virginia: Region Metrics." Coronavirus, Dec. 2020, www.vdh.virginia.gov/coronavirus/key-measures/pandemic-metrics/region-metrics/

[11] United States of America, Center for Disease Control and Prevention. "CDC COVID Data Tracker." Coronavirus Disease 2019 (COVID-19), Dec. 2020 covid.cdc.gov/covid-data-tracker/#popfactors_7daynewcases

humor and casual banter, the two pastors worked hard to push through the technical glitches, including a mis-cue by the Director of Music of a liturgical reading in the middle of the announcements, and to cover their own jittery nerves and frustrations with the limited constraints of the video medium.

After a recorded prelude of rousing piano arrangements of "Holy, Holy, Holy, Lord God Almighty..." and "Christ the Lord is Risen Today, Hallelujah…" and a welcome by the two pastors, Pastor Scott reaffirmed the core elements congregation's vision statement, "to recognize Jesus is on the throne and is worthy of our worship, to disciple one another in the Way of Jesus, and to befriend our neighbors." Restating the PMC vision statement has been a mainstay in the worship services in recent years. However, given the potentially disorienting circumstances, it served as a timely reminder of the congregation's purpose to which they are called, in all seasons.

Being Easter Sunday, the service had a theme of triumph over death and the fear of death. Though the Gospel reading was from John 20:1-18, the resurrection account and Jesus' apparition to Mary Magdalene, the text that most resonated in the sermon came from Hebrews 2:14-15, "Since, therefore, the children share flesh and blood, he himself likewise shared the same things, so that through death he might destroy the one who has the power of death, that is, the devil, and free those who all their lives were held in slavery by the fear of death."[12][13] Pastor Larry, brought the "talk", as he calls it – a five-minute sermonette, composed of four approximately minute-long video segments recorded in different settings.

The opening clip featured an anonymous painting which, Pastor Larry explains, "is of Faust and the devil engaged in a game of chess. The devil holds Faust's queen. Faust's king is in check. An angel observer looks on with little hope. However, a keen eye will notice that Faust has one remaining potential move that can change the fortunes of the game and put his opponent on the defensive." Pastor Larry proposed that the

---

[12] The New Oxford Annotated Bible: With the Apocrypha, Fully Revised Fifth Edition, New Revised Standard Version. Michael D. Coogan, editor. New York: Oxford UP, 2010. Print.

[13] All scripture quotations taken from the New Revised Standard Version (NRSV) unless otherwise noted.

painting is "A metaphor for the Christian life – where at times it seems like, regardless of what we do, death is our end and evil is triumphant. Just as on that fateful Friday, even for Jesus' followers, it seemed as though evil wins – for the Messiah is dead; hope is gone. However, there is but one more move to make – another day is just dawning." The defiant belief that Jesus triumphs over evil held strong.

Though the pandemic was not directly mentioned at all through the entire service, the

context was understood by all who were tuning in from their homes due to the lock down. Pastor Larry honed in on the truth found in Hebrews 2:15 that Jesus sets us free from the fear of death – including our own eventual death, but even more so, the death of a loved one. Trusting assurance in God's triumph over evil and death, and in God's provision of life, "life that death can never take," Pastor Larry explains, "that is faith." He invited the congregation to name those things they are afraid of and to commit them into the full measure of things which Jesus overcame through the resurrection.

Following the "talk", Pastor Scott engaged Pastor Larry in a time of discussion in an effort to apply the sermon. In the weeks leading up to Easter, three congregants had died from reasons unrelated to the pandemic. The congregation had been unable to hold memorial services and to formally grieve together for these well-loved members, or for other friends and relatives who had passed away but were not members of PMC. This was likely the reason Pastor Scott engaged Pastor Larry with the question, "How have you seen people overcome their fear of death well?" Recounting times when a dying congregant was able to do so well, Pastor Larry recounts that, "they would embrace the reality of [their] own death… When they come to peace with that – it's a marvelous inner journey that they take… Also with their loved ones who might not be ready to let them go – they find a way to invite those closest to them into their own journey – so that they can see through that person's eyes… death is no longer frightening, but it becomes welcome. This is going to put an end to those things that I'm dealing with that have made life unlivable." As congregants struggled to find ways of grieving for and releasing deceased loved ones, Pastor Larry sought to offer words of comfort and encouragement to his flock.

However, making peace with one's own death, or that of a loved one, was not the only point that Pastor Larry wanted to make. "Easter morning..." he would declare, "is when we celebrate death's death. What really sets us free from the fear of death is life. It's the promise of life that we receive now in Christ and it's the promise of life that we have for when we enter into death's portal. So, I certainly want to say quite strongly that, this morning, the fear of death is removed in the resurrection of Jesus." The congregation was then led in songs of response which reaffirmed hope in Christ's resurrection and an upbeat declaration that, "Worthy is the King who conquered the grave."[14] No matter what, the church would still exalt the name of Jesus, and trust confidently in his triumph over sin and death, now and forevermore.

April 19, 2020 – Second Sunday of Easter

As Princetown's infection rate climbed by an average of around 41 new cases per 100,000 residents each day[15] (compared to the state-wide rate of 5.5[16] and nation-wide rate of 8.84[17]), PMC gathered remotely for worship once more. A "Zoom-style" video octet of four Singers, each singing two parts, making eight screens of the Harmonia Sacra "Easter Anthem" called the congregation to worship. Riding on the energy of the previous Sunday's Easter theme, much of the music followed the themes of triumph over evil and praising the Lord "The Almighty, the King of Creation," anchoring the congregation's confidence in the sovereignty of God. There was also a defiant irony as the church sang "Here in this Place" and "We Gather Together," though not physically able to gather, thereby sanctifying the unorthodox "space" and way in which the church indeed was gathering. From the onset, the pandemic was named, as

[14] Riddle, Jeremy, et al. "This is Amazing Grace." Phil Wickham Music, 2012.

[15] Commonwealth of Virginia, Virginia Department of Health. "COVID-19 in Virginia: Locality." Coronavirus, Dec. 2020, www.vdh.virginia.gov/coronavirus/key-measures/pandemic-metrics/locality-metrics/

[16] Commonwealth of Virginia, Virginia Department of Health. "COVID-19 in Virginia: Region Metrics." Coronavirus, Dec. 2020, www.vdh.virginia.gov/coronavirus/key-measures/pandemic-metrics/region-metrics/

[17] United States of America, Center for Disease Control and Prevention. "CDC COVID Data Tracker." Coronavirus Disease 2019 (COVID-19), Dec. 2020 covid.cdc.gov/covid-data-tracker/#popfactors_7daynewcases

the congregation was invited to respond to opportunities to contribute masks, finances and other forms of relief for those in need, particularly immigrants, poultry plant workers, and medical personnel in need of child-care assistance. Chat room comments chimed in at different points in the service. The congregation seemed to be admonishing each other not only to make the best of the frustrating limitations, but also to live into what God might surprisingly have for them.

Seminarian Keith, who was carrying out an internship at PMC to fulfill his ministry training requirements, brought a more traditional sermon on the "Road to Emmaus" with the theme "Do you recognize Jesus when you see him?" with a trust toward recognizing the Lord Jesus' character and his ways. Recorded from the church stage pulpit in one continuous clip, Keith drew from Luke 24:13-35, noting that the disciples' expectations for Jesus for the political redemption of Israel had not been met. Hopes shattered, Cleopas and a fellow disciple of Jesus dejectedly and troublingly departed Jerusalem. However, the Lord Jesus met them incognito on that road to Emmaus. Keith wonders if it was the disciples' overconfidence in their certainty about their understanding of scripture and of God's ways, their tying political ideas to scripture, or too strong of a tie to the passions of their lives which caused the disciples not to recognize the Lord when he was right beside them. It was in the breaking of bread, the breaking of the symbol of giving life, that the disciples' eyes were opened to recognize the one who, in allowing himself to be broken, had brought them life. In that moment the disciples' concerns are replaced by the concerns of God and they promptly backtrack to Jerusalem to get back on track with God's Way. Keith exhorted the congregation that it is in times of crisis, when we feel lost and doubtful, and question things we've never questioned before, that we are invited to move closer to the cross, find direction in our relationship to Christ, see Jesus turn our doubts into convictions, renew our minds and open the eyes of our hearts. Practically, Keith called on the congregation to recognize Jesus "in the homeless, the hungry, the thirsty, the sick, the stranger, the prisoner – do you deny yourself to serve them?" The overall feel of the service, though a little less triumphant, was more resolute – to not only endure the challenging times, but to respond in grace to the needs around the congregation. The service closed with "Be Thou My Vision," inviting the Lord to adjust the congregation's perceptions to be in harmony with God's reality.

April 26, 2020 – Third Sunday of Easter

Having reached the spring's peak infection rate of a disturbing 7-day average of 60 new cases per 100,000 residents on April 23, Princetown's infection rate dropped to an average of around 36 new cases per 100,000 residents each day[18] (compared to the state-wide rate of 7.4[19] and nation-wide rate of 9.09[20]), PMC congregants once more gathered for worship from their own homes. The song of choice was "Amazing Grace", presented three times instrumentally, a cappella, and in praise and worship style throughout the service. Notable also was the presentation of "All Will be Well", authored by Black Plague survivor Julian of Norwich, a congregational song confessing the Lord's promise to care and shepherd his people through dark times.

Pastor Larry was back on the screens with a sermon on the book of Job, with which he would open a new sermon series entitled "Hope Remains" which would run through June 1st. In this sermon, which flitted from one setting to another, Pastor Larry would articulate clearly a theology of suffering and of grace, in response to the pandemic. Asking the question "Does the good we do any good?" Pastor Larry would challenge the congregation not to yield to an interpretation of negative events as being caused by particular sin. Evil is present in the world.

The world is the theater for the struggle between good and evil. Everyone, regardless of the righteousness of their actions, is touched by the effects of evil. Nevertheless, God is present with us in our suffering. The Lead Pastor implored the congregation not to try to find someone to blame for evil, as Job's friends did. Instead, Pastor Larry dared his flock to hope, because when we dare to hope, it leads to a revelation of God's goodness. Doing good deeds does not protect us from evil, but it is a sign of God's goodness, which will bring hope to others. With this challenge

---

[18] Commonwealth of Virginia, Virginia Department of Health. "COVID-19 in Virginia: Locality." Coronavirus, Dec. 2020, www.vdh.virginia.gov/coronavirus/key-measures/pandemic-metrics/locality-metrics/

[19] Commonwealth of Virginia, Virginia Department of Health. "COVID-19 in Virginia: Region Metrics." Coronavirus, Dec. 2020, www.vdh.virginia.gov/coronavirus/key-measures/pandemic-metrics/region-metrics/

[20] United States of America, Center for Disease Control and Prevention. "CDC COVID Data Tracker." Coronavirus Disease 2019 (COVID-19), Dec. 2020 covid.cdc.gov/covid-data-tracker/#popfactors_7daynewcases

to acknowledge the presence of God in our suffering, and to choose to bring hope to others through good deeds, Pastor Larry called on his congregation to engage however the Spirit might lead in the struggle between good and evil, which constantly rages in the world, whether more or less obviously. Our good deeds are not futile. They are a means to impart hope.

May 3, 2020 – Fourth Sunday of Easter

As Princetown's infection rate dropped slightly to an average of around 28 new cases per 100,000 residents each day[21] (compared to the state-wide rate of 9.6[22] and nation-wide rate of 8.34[23]), PMC gathered remotely for worship once more. By this point, the stay at home order had lasted over a month. The staff assembled a video and photo collage, entitled "Separate… but not apart", of contributions from congregants on how they have been spending their time. Activities included photos of blooming trees, gardening in a greenhouse, a Saturday morning pancake fry, jokes about shaggy appearances due to the closure of hair salons, family outings, two youth who walked a marathon together, ending with the words "In this together!" These montages would become prominent features in PMC's video services.

Music Director Jon gave a moving rendition of "Come, ye disconsolate" with the refrain "Here bring your wounded hearts, here tell your anguish. Earth has no sorrows that Heav'n cannot heal". Indeed, the feel of the service was somber, as a nearby nursing home, where PMC had often made the focus of outreaches through the years, had experienced a major outbreak that would result in the deaths of over twenty residents.

---

[21] Commonwealth of Virginia, Virginia Department of Health. "COVID-19 in Virginia: Locality." Coronavirus, Dec. 2020, www.vdh.virginia.gov/coronavirus/key-measures/pandemic-metrics/locality-metrics/

[22] Commonwealth of Virginia, Virginia Department of Health. "COVID-19 in Virginia: Region Metrics." Coronavirus, Dec. 2020, www.vdh.virginia.gov/coronavirus/key-measures/pandemic-metrics/region-metrics/

[23] United States of America, Center for Disease Control and Prevention. "CDC COVID Data Tracker." Coronavirus Disease 2019 (COVID-19), Dec. 2020 covid.cdc.gov/covid-data-tracker/#popfactors_7daynewcases

Another feature of the service was an interview that Pastor Scott did of Jenny, a Latina mother of three young children, who has led holistic outreaches in her minority-majority neighborhood for years. Jenny shared about how her family had been able to adjust from previous patterns of outreach to new strategies of engagement. Whereas in previous years, dozens of children would descend on their house over Holy Week and other special events, this year her family knocked on neighbors' doors on Palm Sunday "with a Bluetooth speaker playing music and dancing around like fools." She recounted how on Easter Sunday they partnered with three churches to assemble and deliver baskets with treats, a craft, a book, snacks and a $25 grocery card. Prayer walks through the neighborhood continued as before. She shared about particular challenges her neighbors experience in this time, many of them being affected more acutely by both the virus and the economic downturn brought on by the lock-down. However, she stressed that "we have a lot to learn from our refugee and immigrant neighbors about resilience in the face of trauma… [responding in] faithfulness, generosity and hospitality."

Pastor Scott brought the message, continuing with the "Hope Remains" theme. Conducting a word study on the theme of hope in Joshua 7:24-26, Hosea 2:15 and John 10:7-10, he concluded that "Hope isn't an idea or a doctrine – it's a person named Jesus, always with us in the valley of trouble." He reminded the congregation of Jesus' presence with them in this dark valley and exhorted the flock to remain present to Jesus – "seeking him, opening up your lives to him, making space for him, listening to him." He encouraged the church to draw life from Jesus in the scriptures, in prayer, in his community, in the presence of the sick, impoverished and lonely. In the throes of a very difficult time in the community, Pastor Scott issued a clear call not to yield to hopelessness brought on by the stress, anxiety, isolation and despair which were rampant in their community, but to choose to draw from the light and life of Jesus in order to make a positive impact.

Pastoral Approach

Challenging though it was, the transition to worshiping remotely has likely proven to be the simplest one experienced by the congregation. Pastor Larry spoke for the staff when he said, "We want our old jobs back, because we're not very good at our new jobs." Leadership has proven to be one of the more difficult tasks to carry out in this pandemic. Far more takes place on a usual Sunday morning and throughout the week in a church's life than merely gathering on Sundays. However, the restrictions on gathering brought on by the pandemic have meant that informal occasions, such as lingering conversations in the parking lot after gatherings, are no longer as likely to take place.

As the stay at home order began, the pastoral staff recognized early on the potential for isolation among more vulnerable congregants. Christina, a single day care teacher who joined PMC in her young adult years, told me of how the staff divided up the directory each week, with each staff member contacting at least ten people a day to get through the directory. Christina noted, "It's fallen off since then… but at the beginning, I was getting calls from the staff weekly." Pastor Larry shared that he has never spent so much time conversing and praying over the phone in his 38 years as a pastor. He noted as time passed, congregants started recognizing his phone number and answering more readily than at first. As the stay-at-home order wore on, the phone calls continued, but in a more targeted manner, which focused especially on families in difficulty or transition. Particularly with hospitalizations and illness, those times when a pastoral visit would have been a given, the phone call or text was the only way to reach out.

Aside from phone calls and text messaging, mailed correspondence played a key role in maintaining the values of community and fellowship. For Christina, cards became an important way to receive care and to express it. Through regular cards and occasional gifts from various members of the congregation, Christina experienced the church reaching out to her in tangible ways. When one of the church staff approached her about sending cards to people in nursing homes, Christina was delighted. "I must have made and sent out forty or cards to people," she shared proudly, "more than I've made in the past twenty years!" Christina came to see this as way for her to make sure that those who were most isolated would know that "Somebody's thinking of me!" A call one day confirmed her conviction. As the caller shared, through tears, that "'after reading an email with all these regulations, when I was feeling discouraged, I received your card.' This encouraged me too!" beamed Christina. "I sent her another card."

After the Virginia stay-at-home order lifted on May 15, it took some time for the church to discern how best to move forward. Though they technically were allowed to gather in-person, they would only be able to use the church building at 50% capacity, maintaining six feet distance, masked and with no singing – a preposterous idea for a community which prides itself in resounding four-part a cappella singing! Perhaps the most restrictive stipulation, however, would prove to be the cleaning measures required after any use of the building. In a June 4 email to the congregation, Assistant Pastor Scott noted that "At this point, the stringent cleaning requirements are still applicable and prohibitively expensive and time consuming" for congregants to use the church building. However, Pastor Scott's email encouraged Sunday School classes to gather in person outside or indoors in small groups with masks, physical distancing of six feet, and without singing. Up to this point, some classes had already begun to gather via Zoom video conference calls, "But," Pastor Scott exhorted, "we need to be together, and not simply on Zoom. We need each other's presence, need to see the language that cannot be communicated merely by words. Added to this is a broken, unjust, violent world that desperately needs the church to be the church, to follow Jesus well, to be present in ways that are helpful and beautiful, not harmful and divisive...The size of group is actually incredibly helpful in fostering discipleship," wrote Pastor Scott. "The ancient biblical scholars, drawing from the text, believed a congregation began at 10 people. Jesus himself chose to disciple 12, though he had thousands more disciples." Sunday School classes were again proving to be the backbone of PMC and the core expression of the church, aside from the nuclear family, through which the congregation might be able to reengage in key formative rituals.

Through the sermons and video worship gatherings, the pastoral staff articulated a clear theology of grace and hope in the midst of suffering. Through the accounts of Jesus' death and resurrection, the encounter on the Emmaus Road, the story of Job, and Jesus' call for his people to acknowledge his sovereign presence with them in all circumstances, the community of PMC was invited to trust in God's Way, shun escapism and bitterness, and engage with good deeds, in order to be agents of God's Kingdom in a world which was suffering. The call for missional engagement rang clear through email announcements, word-of-mouth invitations, and from the screens – God is with you and can use you for good in this dark time.

Congregational Response

On the effects of the pandemic on the congregation, Pastor Larry stated, "It's hard to know how this is shaking down." While many other congregations were able to return to some form of in-person worship gathering, PMC chose to remain mainly remote. While there was an initial push to have some watch the sermon together in the church sanctuary, local outbreaks caused that effort to stop. As of the writing of this article, PMC has yet to resume in-person gatherings. When I spoke with Heather, life-long PMC member and mother of two teenage and college-age children, she shared that her family had begun to worship elsewhere. Due to the remote worshiping, she had started exploring other local churches, even while contributing to various video elements of PMC's services. Her mention of the importance her Sunday School class continued to have for her and her husband underscored the inadequacy of "remote fellowship" and the "spectator approach" of PMC's YouTube services. While YouTube viewing rates have held steady at around 500 views per week, it is hard to know how many members will not be reconnecting with PMC when in-person worship resumes. Pastor Larry stated, "Those who want to stay connected have worked hard to do so. Weak connections have gotten weaker."

Ritual has certainly suffered. Aside from weekly worship gatherings, including the sharing of communion, physical separation has taken its toll on key benchmark events, such as child dedications, baptisms, including pre-baptism catechesis, marriages and funerals. PMC has long had the tradition of holding baptisms on Easter Sunday. This year, none took place over Easter, with a quiet, single baptism being the only one so far this year. Though memorial services were initially postponed, most have been canceled, with little hope that they will eventually be held. Some losses cannot be entirely recovered.

Post-Pandemic Future

Through diverse creative forms of Sunday School and youth gatherings, Christian formation continues. There is little concern among PMC's leadership that this pandemic will cripple the church in any way, though the membership may contract some. Pastor Larry indicated that he believes the convenience of gathering remotely will cause administrative meetings to remain remote, to some degree. However, if there is anything that this pandemic has taught people, it is the value of being together, in the flesh – "with unveiled faces". Given the opportunity, the community of believers at PMC, regardless of demographic, will be eager to gather physically. Intimacy is far more precious than convenience.

Reflections & the *Missio Dei*

As the "church in the city," PMC strives to present faithful Anabaptist expressions of Christian faith that are contextually relevant to broader society. Mission, expressed through service and evangelism, is a central value, emerging through countless formal and informal expressions of the church, at the individual, congregational, denominational, and interdenominational levels. In normal times, many members engage in cross-cultural short-term and long-term missions through Mennonite and broader mission agencies. PMC also engages in local and national ministries, with their focus being on ending homelessness, community counseling, building housing for low-income families, and providing support to immigrants.

Among PMC's mission endeavors are projects to steward the church's campus, located at the top of a hill in a city subdivision in a way that reflects hospitality and care for creation. The intent is to make the campus available in a way that serves the neighboring community and promotes relationship between the community and PMC members, many of whom do not live in that community. This finds expression in a community garden, with about forty small plots available for community and congregational members to cultivate side-by-side, including through monthly potluck meals in the warmer months. The development of a handicapped accessible meditation path around the property's perimeter, intentionally planted with native species by a PMC member, who is a career botanist, also seeks to contribute positively in the community. Along with a playground and an athletic field, these features make the church grounds an active space throughout the week, year-round. In *Churches that Make a Difference: Reaching Your Community with Good News and Good Works*, Ronald Sider, et al., outline three basic components to the church's mission: "[witnessing] to God's kingdom by proclaiming the Good News of Christ," "not only [pointing] to God's coming kingdom but [being] an example of its inception," and "[serving] as a sign of God's kingdom by modeling the Good News in the community of faith."[24] PMC's multi-faceted strategies of evangelism and social engagement, which include the neighborhood immediately surrounding the church campus and the broader community, in addition to a national and international level, reflects the kind of commitment to community outreach necessary for true holistic witness to the Good News of Jesus Christ in our world.

In the life of the church there are seasons. There are seasons of investing, of preparing the soil and planting. There are seasons of harvest, of gathering in, and rejoicing. There also seasons of pruning, of evaluating, and of drawing deeply through our roots from the soil. This has been a season of pruning. The church has been stripped of so much of what it may have previously thought was essential. The church has been charged with evaluating what is truly central to its existence. The church has needed to evaluate what will remain and what can be released, even if just for a season. The church has been reminded that, as long as it maintains a steadfast connection to the source of life, even when it seems like all life has been drained away, a new spring will come, and the life which was there all along will again be evidenced by new growth. As the Lord Jesus taught his disciples, "Abide in me as I abide in you. Just as the branch cannot bear fruit by itself unless it abides in the vine, neither can you unless you abide in me." If nothing else, this time apart has given the church opportunity to draw deeply from the Lord. Those who have taken advantage of this time to do so will emerge all the stronger for it.

Despite the challenges the church faces, even in this period of pruning, God has been doing God's work through God's people in the

---

[24] Sider, Ronald J., et al. *Churches that Make a Difference: Reaching Your Community with Good News and Good Works* (Ada, Michigan: Baker Books, 2005), 148.

world, in spite of the church's limitations in doing so. Christina testified to this, as she shared with me of one of the only Sundays that she failed to tune in to PMC's online service. As is her habit, she had gone for a morning prayer walk through her neighborhood, stopping particularly in front of the houses of other PMC members she knew to pray over their households. That morning, as she prayed in front of the home of one PMC couple where both husband and wife are registered nurses in the local hospital, she recognized an inner nudge to knock on their door. Upon answering the door, the wife shared with Christina, who is in the same Sunday School class, that just that morning, their garage had been vandalized. Flammable liquid had been poured everywhere and much of the contents of the garage were in disarray. Evidently there had been a pattern of vandalism in their neighborhood. Her husband had needed to leave for his shift on the COVID-19 patient ward just before Christina arrived. Christina and her friend donned masks as they began working together to clean up the mess, praying as they labored. That was the last instance of vandalism in thatneighborhood. A pattern of evil was broken through a willingness to follow God's agenda, to pray in faith, and to physically engage in cleaning up the mess. Indeed, our good deeds do impart hope, and hope will remain. God continues to choose to use God's people in surprising ways to accomplish his purposes.

Case Study Thirteen: Despite Everything… God is Still in Control

Hartlen Coats

Hartlen Coats has pastored 12 churches, including 2 years on the mission field. He also spent 5 years in Christian radio ministry and has engaged in itinerant ministry. He and his wife, Dianne, reside in a suburb of Tulsa, OK, where he is Founder/President of Hartlen G. Coats Ministries.

Context: Suburban Oklahoma
Affiliation: Small Charismatic Denomination
Size: 75 average attendance

Introduction

This report is a brief study of a local church and its response to the Covid-19 pandemic. It studies the church's actions during a period of being closed, as well as afterwards. It includes feedback from interviews with the Lead Pastor and two congregational members. As part of the study, I reviewed online live streaming services before, during, and after the period when the church was closed. As a former member, pastoral staff member, and personal friend of the Lead Pastor, I will be adding some behind the scenes insights.

Church Context

New Life Church is located in a medium-sized city in Oklahoma, and is housed in one of its major suburbs. The pre-pandemic attendance averaged seventy-five, with a contemporary, charismatic worship style. It is a member of a small charismatic denomination. The governance was pastor-led with a corporate board for legal decisions. The Lead Pastor is the only paid employee and other pastoral staff serve on a voluntary basis. He is thirty-eight years old, married, has two children and attended a two-year Bible school. He was the Youth Pastor for many years and had also worked for the denomination for a time. The church is sixty to seventy percent Millennials and other young adults, with the remainder being Boomers.

The city is known for its Christian population and schools. It is home to several Bible schools, two Christian universities with seminaries (one denominational and one independent), and multiple satellite classes of both in-state and out-of-state Christian, state, and private colleges and universities. It has a reputation for being or having been the home of several high-profile charismatic ministers, with a plethora of charismatic ministries and churches still located in the city. There are multiple mega churches, both denominational and non-denominational. Most would say that the state would be considered as part of the Midwestern Bible Belt.

New Life Church was located in Oklahoma, which was about two months behind New York and other places that were hard hit by the pandemic. The governor did not restrict crowds, nor require face masks. He only required face masks in state government offices in August when a spike started to occur. There were no serious restrictions in this state until September, when schools began. Schools met in person until late October, when they were forced into online only learning in the large cities in the state.

In deciding when to close and reopen, Lead Pastor Paul said they did take clues from other churches locally and in other states. They especially payed attention to the mega churches in their city, as well as other churches in their own suburb. Because they are part of a small denomination that leaves the local church autonomous, they had very little guidance from the hierarchy as to what to do. The advice they received was to pray and use wisdom regarding staying open or closing. Some churches in their small denomination were defiant to government orders and stayed open, some closed sooner. It had a lot to do with the part of the country they were in and the leadership of the pastor.

Church Response & Social Media

The church closed and went to strictly online services on March 22, 2020 and returned to regular services in the building on June 21, 2020. They had been livestreaming on their YouTube channel for several years, and this is the platform they used for sermons while not meeting in person. They recorded these sermons and premiered them on YouTube. They were already using Instagram and Facebook for communication and announcements, as well as a mass text message program which was also used during this time. With the high percentage of Millennials, the communication via social media and texting worked very well. Even most of the Boomers were on some social platform, so communication via social media worked well.

In addition, the Lead Pastor did an informal live Facebook broadcast every Wednesday Evening, combining interviews and short devotionals. While they had good response, they were discontinued after the church went back to live services. They continued with the YouTube online streaming after the church reopened, as well as using the other platforms for communication. However, they never did stream their services on other social media platforms, such as Facebook, and stayed with the YouTube platform throughout the pandemic.

According to Pastor Paul, they originally thought that they would only be closed for a month. Because of this, they provided an informal devotional style of message for Sunday mornings. When they could see that the pandemic was going to last longer, they did more formal messages, based on themes of the season and included members of the worship team presenting a few songs. From this, we see that the church changed its strategy mid-stream, as did other churches.

Pastor Paul said they did discover that one of their weaknesses was that they had let their social media platforms fall into little usage. They corrected this during this period by having the communications director schedule regular communications, rather than random posting. They attempted to make a better connection with the congregation, as well as communicate when services would be made available.

On the first online-only sermon, the pandemic was addressed directly with encouragement that God was not responsible and would see people through the crisis. As time passed, the pandemic was addressed less and less, so that, even during Easter season and post- Easter season, the pandemic was only mentioned in passing. Most of the sermons were directed at personal experience and God's comfort and support, which was applied indirectly to the pandemic, but just passing references to the pandemic itself.

This was influenced by the theological stance of the denomination, which believes that God is good and does not cause calamity or tragedy. These things happen because we live in a fallen world, the lack of following God's Word, a lack a faith, or demonic intervention. In the case of the pandemic, God was with each believer, to comfort and strengthen them, in spite of what was going on around them. The pandemic was attributed to living in a fallen world and circumstances beyond anyone's control. God was certainly not responsible, but certainly was the answer through comforting Christians and providing healing.

Pastor Paul's theology of the pandemic matched the denominational view, and was reflected in his sermons of comfort and encouragement. During the post-Easter time the Sunday sermons were divided among the entire staff including the Lead Pastor, Administrative Pastor, Youth Pastor, Children's Pastor, and Communications Director. During this time, they also experimented with using a traditional liturgical calendar to determine Scripture readings and sermon topics, beginning with Easter and ending with the Fourth Sunday of Easter. Again, the sermons did not directly address the pandemic, but mentioned it in passing. All the sermons were aimed at helping listeners experience the peace and love of God.

Pastor Paul and the staff did take this time to evaluate some of their theological positions and consider alternate church structure. They were already in an evaluative mode, reviewing some doctrine, vision, and structure, when the pandemic broke out. One of their major discussions was to determine what practices and processes they had in place that were the result of the denominational and theological culture and tradition. Pastor Paul was only the third pastor and the church had been started by a high-profile minister that was the head of their denomination. Although he had died, children had taken over the church and Pastor Paul took over the church from them. Most of the traditions and practices of the church had remained unchanged since its founding. The staff thought that this might be part of the reason the church was not growing.

The pastoral staff and leaders tried to identify traditions that were passed down that were still in the church. There was a constant pull from the Boomers to remain the same and follow the dictates of the founder, while Millennials were constantly wanting to move in more contemporary directions and practices. Being closed gave the staff a chance to examine everything and reevaluate their practices and procedures without the influence of the congregational factions. They discussed several different structural and organizational changes and, thinking outside the box, even considered going to an online only church in the future.

During the pandemic, as noted above, the state where the church was located did not have the restrictions imposed to the degree that other states did. Pastor Paul was able to carry on pastoral care in much the same way as before. He had two people hospitalized during this time, including the birth of a baby. He was able to visit as usual during the early part of the pandemic.

One of the church's most active ministries has always been the Hospitality Ministry. One major function of this ministry was to organize meals to be served any time to members who were in the hospital, had a death in the family, or any other similar crisis. It also organized things like babysitting and donations of clothes, money, and other items for families in hardship. During the pandemic, the Hospitality Ministry continued providing meals for members. However, there was a different twist, due to people wanting to refrain from contact with each other. So, those who participated used DoorDash, or other food delivery services, to provide the meals. It was the perfect example of the church adapting to the situation in a creative way. Another unique form of ministry happened on Mother's Day. The pastoral staff prepared gift baskets for mothers and delivered them to their homes on Mother's Day morning.

Providing a personal touch, in lieu of services, was a challenge faced by all churches that were shut-down. New Life Church stayed in touch by taking the congregation and dividing it into small groups among the pastoral staff and leaders. Each week, they would call or text the people in their group to check on them, offer encouragement, and pray for them. The church also continued the Prayer Chain ministry, so that members could continue to pray for each other. The staff felt that this helped people have a sense of staying connected and contributing significantly to the ministry of the church.

As mentioned above, Pastor Paul hosted a Facebook live session on Wednesday evenings. These sessions proved to be very successful, as people were able to interact directly with him and any guests, as well as others watching and commenting. People were invited to comment on the theme of the night, answer a poll question, or interact with guests or others who were watching. It was a very effective way to allow people to interact and feel connected to each other and the church.

Congregational Response

The pandemic brought many changes in the world on many different levels. New Life Church also experienced many changes both during being closed and after they reopened. Pastor Paul observed that while they were closed, they were surprised how many people who were watching online actually interacted during the live broadcast. They were also surprised about how their viewing numbers were low, compared to what live service attendance had been.

The other change that took place during the time when they were closed was the number of people that decided not to attend the church any longer. Most of the people that did not return notified Pastor Paul during this time. The church was already struggling somewhat and it seemed that not having live services gave some people the feeling that it was all right to go ahead and leave the church. In talking with them, they discovered that most of them were already thinking about leaving the church. Several of them were a real surprise to the pastor and the staff, as they had been with the church many years and some were in leadership roles.

After returning to live services, there were also some surprising changes in the congregation. Pastor Paul was amazed to see how divided the congregation was on social issues. At least one couple left the church over the racism issue, as the Assistant Pastor was black and shared about racism in the online service shortly after the George Floyd incident. Like most churches, many people were wary of attending, so the attendance was lower than it would have been had there not been a pandemic. The wearing of masks was quite an issue for some. Remember, the state they were in was not requiring the wearing of masks or restricting crowds. There were some in the congregation that felt that the wearing of masks was part of a government conspiracy to restrict civil liberties.

Alice is a professional in her mid-forties who has her own home-based business. She had been very involved in the church several years ago, until she worked overseas for over a year. Upon her return and with her business, she was less involved, although she did still do some volunteer work. Even though less involved, she still had close connections with people in the congregation, including some of her own family members. She felt the online services were already helping her feel connected, even before the pandemic, when she was not able to attend services. Alice did watch the online services each week while the church was closed. She said it was important to her to hear what the pastor was sharing, so that she could stay full of the Word, in addition to her own studies.

Alice also watched other church services online during the pandemic. This was actually a practice she had before the pandemic. She watches several high-profile ministers on television and likes to follow along when they do a series on a topic. So, this was not a new practice due to the pandemic. She felt that listening to other ministers helped her be more rounded as a Christian. Listening to these ministers helped fill gaps that she might have.

It is interesting to note that she did not realize how much not having physical church services affected her until she returned in person. She says, "the support I have from the people in the church and communicating with them on a weekly basis was what I was missing, and I didn't even realize it." She felt that others were also experiencing this "emotional and spiritual distancing."

Alice delayed returning to the physical services to protect a nephew that was in a high-risk health category. She quarantined completely for two months. This, combined with the isolation from church, did cause some anxiety and she even had to fight off depression. She felt that if she could have been with either family or attended church, it would have been easier on her and she would not have struggled so much. Once the family felt safe getting together again and she was able to return to church, her depression and loneliness subsided.

For Alice, God's role in the pandemic related more to her personal life rather than the overall worldwide experience. She did not see that God had any part in causing the pandemic. She experienced some panic and anxiety at first, but after recognizing this, she became more diligent in maintaining her daily spiritual disciplines.

She saw a negative effect of the pandemic on New Life Church. The church closed for good after returning to live services (see Epilogue). Alice felt that this was caused by the drop in attendance after live services began. She also thought that the reason some of the families left was because other churches opened sooner than New Life Church. This was the opinion of several members, yet there were more factors involved. It was a logical conclusion to draw and she saw the church closing down due to the pandemic as a major factor.

While crises like the pandemic sometimes makes people question their faith, Alice's theological view of God did not change. She held with the denominational view that God is good, and the pandemic did not come from God. Instead, it caused her to be more concerned about the needs of others. She says, "It makes me realize how many people in this world are still lost and need Him."

Alice felt the pastor and staff adapted well to being restricted to the online services. Since she was already taking advantage of the livestreaming, it was just normal to continue. They did have technical problems several times, especially when they added a worship team and the videos got longer. Alice says that the pastor and staff communicated through social media and texts to let people know what was happening. She did not see this as a negative, but appreciated the fact that they were communicating with people.

During the time the church was closed, Alice says that the team leader from her volunteer area texted or called regularly. The pastor also contacted her via text messages. She really enjoyed the Wednesday night Facebook live sessions with the pastor, where she could join in and communicate with him and others who were watching. Alice felt that the pastor, staff, and leadership did an excellent job of reaching out to her and other church members. This was comforting, and she did appreciate it. However, it was still no substitute for in-person contact, which she felt was vital for her personally and for the church.

Linda is in her mid-fifties and works at the denominational headquarters. She has been the church secretary and treasurer for many years. She also serves on the corporate board and on the leadership team, overseeing a couple of areas of the church. She watched the online services every week while the church was closed. As she held several positions in the church, she had a high level of commitment and watching online was normal.

She did not watch services from other churches, as she felt it wasn't necessary, since she was getting what she needed from her own pastor. Linda was a graduate of a well-known Bible school in town and is very mature. She is of the opinion that if your church is feeding you Properly, then there is no need to seek other places to receive the Word. Also, being a Boomer, loyalty and commitment are part of her norms.

Linda is very much a people person and being away from others in the congregation while being closed was a challenge. She not only missed seeing people, her emotional make-up caused it to be a struggle not to see people and "give hugs." Because the worship style of the church is contemporary charismatic, it was a large part of what makes church very meaningful for her. Not being able to engage in corporate worship was one of the things that she felt affected her the most. Even though some of the online services included worship, it was not the same as being with the church family and experiencing worship together.

Returning to the live services was an easy move for Linda. She says, "I like going to in-person services; it was an easy decision to make. I went as soon as it opened." Again, their state was behind others in the outbreak of the pandemic and their governor did not have restrictions on groups when they went back to live services. She didn't really sense any danger and the church did make provisions for some social distancing in seating. Most people seemed to feel safe and there was little concern about the spread of the pandemic due to live services.

Linda is in accord with the denominational view that God is good and does not cause calamity. This is also the theological position of the Bible school she attended. When questioned about God's role in the pandemic, she says, "God is a good God. His role is health, healing, and providing for the needs of people." Her view was that God was not responsible for the pandemic and his role was one of protection and healing. She felt that God had the answers for the pandemic and was not the cause of the pandemic. The pandemic did not change her view of God in any way.

Linda was sure that the church would close permanently, even though they reopened. She felt the pandemic was a significant factor, but not the only factor. The church did close after the pandemic (see Epilogue). Being part of the inner circle, Linda could already see this coming. She understood the financial position of the church, was aware of the struggles of the pastor, and was aware of the loss of members. It was somewhat inevitable, from her point of view, that the church would close soon, even after they began live services again.

Linda felt that the pastor adapted very well to moving to an online only format. She says, "He responded quickly and came up with a plan for online services right away. There was no delay in our services." Being part of the Executive Team for ministry and planning, she knew how quickly the pastor had reacted. She trusted his guidance and, being part of the leadership team, helped with some of the planning.

Linda reiterated what Alice said about being contacted by the church on a weekly basis. She not only received communication, but was part of the leadership team that was making calls and texts to check up on people. This meant she was being cared for directly by the pastor and also sharing in caring for the congregation. She felt that helping care for the congregation was not only important, but that she was receiving the greater blessing for doing so.

Epilogue: Impact on the Future of the Congregation

Unfortunately, New Life Church did close permanently, and had their final service on October 18, 2020. Pastor Paul had tendered his resignation a few weeks before this and the Board recognized that it was time to bring things to an end. The decline in membership and loss of revenue, along with the general lack of enthusiasm, were all determining factors. While most people thought it was the result of Covid-19, the pandemic could only be considered a catalyst that caused multiple factors to come together to cause the closing.

Pastor Paul had taken over a church that had been a family operation, started by a high-profile minister, and had lots of high expectations for a pastor. Pastor Paul had been the Youth Pastor for a number of years, and there were high hopes that he could revive an already struggling church. He faced a declining membership, heavy debt, and an unclear direction for the church.

As mentioned before, there were different factions pulling in different directions. Nobody could live up to the original pastor's performance, but the Boomers were looking for someone to restore the church to its former glory. Millennials and the younger set were wanting to pull away from the denominational traditions and long engrained ideas of what the church should look like. With this wavering back and forth, it was difficult, at best, to present a new vision and path for the church. Before the pandemic shut-down, the church was already losing some membership and could not get enough traction for positive momentum. The pandemic shut-down was perhaps simply an easier time for people to leave, as the commitments to attendance and service were not necessary.

Pastoral Response

One of the things that came out of the pandemic shut-down was Pastor Paul's realization that he was nearing burnout. Reflecting on the time off, he says, "I also believe, like myself, ministers are faced with what's really going on in their lives and family, as the pressure to pastor only increased in this season." During this time, he entered into therapy, which helped him examine himself more deeply. Being home so much and away from the office, he had time to reflect on life and do some personal evaluation. He recognized the toll that pastoring under these circumstances took on himself, his marriage, and his children. This was the determining factor for his resignation.

He did offer some reflections on how the pandemic changed the way he sees ministry. He says, "I believe even more in connecting with people online. I was surprised at how many people grew closer to Jesus with online availability. However, I also believe even more in connecting in person. I am now more of a 'both' rather than an 'either/or.'" This is an important shift in his thinking, as one of his strongest traits was the ability to connect one-on-one and face-to-face, in order to mentor and disciple people.

He also reflected on his thoughts about long-term effects of how the pandemic might change the way church is done in the future. He says, "It's interesting to think how much creativity was unlocked in churches." He noted that his own leadership team came up with innovative ways to perform ministry, in spite of abnormal circumstances. He says, "I believe that churches who were against livestreaming, will now continually offer it." He noted that many churches were forced into livestreaming and discovered that it was a good tool for ministering to their own congregations, as well as a form of outreach. It helped to bring many churches into the digital age that were opposed to it before. It also taught them how easy it is and how inexpensive. It was a great training opportunity for many older ministers to see the importance of social media and the use of technology.

Pastor Paul pointed out that the overhead from having an unusable building was eye opening for himself and churches in general. He says, "Those who have high overhead, will look for ways to creatively use their facilities and possibly venture into for-profits." He pointed out a fellow minister whose church owns a facility and rents part of that facility to businesses, which covers the overhead for the church. He brought out that there are numerous examples of churches involved in similar for-profit ventures, that provide a financial security for those churches.

Finally, Pastor Paul commented on how he feels the pandemic might change the theological approach of churches. He says, "I also believe that there will become a more basic gospel, returning to a more holistic gospel approach in ministry." He felt that the pandemic had forced him to begin looking at the basic needs of people, rather than trying to focus on teaching theology. The pandemic revealed how people are really hurting and the shut-down simply compounded that for them. It forced people to realize how fragile they were and how much they need to be strong in the Gospel. It also helped ministers to focus more on making disciples, rather than simply dispensing theology and denominational doctrine.

Reflections & the *Missio Dei*

The story of what New Life Church and Pastor Paul experienced during the pandemic and the shut-down period bring to light several ideas that might be common in many churches. The focus of the local church should be the *Missio Dei*, God's mission, which should reflect God's initiative and guidance.[1] The *Missio Dei* for the local church should be driven by God, rather than by our own efforts, denominational preferences, or personal desires.

In the case of New Life Church, it seems that there were too many influences trying to determine what the church should look like in mission. Most of the focus of the church seemed to be internal and which generation would have the influence. Pastor Paul and the staff were on the right track to be evaluating where they were and where they should go. However, it was probably too late, with the pandemic shutting down live church services.

The mission of the church should be looking toward the future, not the past.[2] The Boomers should have been looking more toward the future of the church, rather than looking to the past and wanting to return to the glory days. This is a form of self-satisfaction and self-indulgence, rather than selfless sacrifice. Christopher Wright says that, "our mission flows from God's mission, and God's mission is for the sake of the

---

[1] Robert Gallagher and Paul Hertig, *Landmark Essays in Mission and World Christianity: 43* (Orbis Books: Kindle Edition, 2009) 13-14.

[2] Christopher Wright, *The Mission of God's People* (Zondervan: Apple Books, 2010), 22.

whole world."[3] While you need good structure, doctrine, and internal systems, the primary focus of the church should be on how to fulfill God's mission in the world. The struggle over what the church should look like internally may have caused interference, making it difficult to look beyond the internal situation. There needed to be a missional focus for people of all generations to rally around and give them all some common ground where they could work together for a cause.

Pastor Paul alluded to the *Missio Dei* in his remarks about what he learned about the importance of online services reaching outside the church. He says, "I think of Jesus' ministry, how we see him with his disciples and with the crowds. In one instance, he went to Tyre and Sidon. These cities were so far away, and even considered to be 'out of the way', both socially and theologically. However, because of the mission to touch the whole house of Israel, Jesus goes there once. In providing online services, it gives the people in 'Tyre and Sidon' the opportunity to be reached." This seems to be an indicator that Pastor Paul was beginning to look outside the church and into the world. The pause caused by the pandemic gave him this opportunity. Looking at the internal struggles seemed to have caused him to be preoccupied with the internal concerns in the church and distracted from looking outward to the world.

Another issue that caused too much of an internal focus was some of the pressures on Pastor Paul. He expressed the thought that he felt pressure to bring the church back to life. There certainly was this type of pressure from multiple sources, both inside the church and from the denomination. After all, he was the exciting Youth Pastor and had worked for the denomination for a few years, creating a youth ministry for them. His successes in that area were reason to believe that he could be the one to bring the church out of the downward spiral it had been in for several years.

He was well liked in the church and people responded to him well. However, having to focus on bringing a dying church back to life, along with heavy debt, were indeed ominous obstacles, no matter who you were. Added to this pressure was the fact that this was supposed to be the "Mother Church" for the denomination, where failure was not an option. Rather than having the freedom to focus on the *Missio Dei,*

---

[3] Wright, 22.

Pastor Paul was forced to focus on everything except the *Missio Dei.* God's mission had to take no more than equal billing with the rest of these pressures and never seems to have had the opportunity to come to the forefront.

This type of situation is played out over and over in churches around the world. I acknowledge the importance of assuring that the local church and its functions need attention. Part of the pastor's role is to guide the internal functions and care of members through the internal systems. However, when survival becomes the main focus, or worse - the only focus, then the *Missio Dei* takes a back seat and sometimes is forgotten altogether. When survival becomes the only purpose of a church, then it is possible that its focus on survival is what will prevent that very survival that is sought.

Survival mode is not exciting, and can even be frightening. When you are focused on survival mode and internal issues, then you are not focused on the *Missio Dei* and a world needing the Gospel. Proverbs 29:18 says, "Where there is no vision, the people perish: but he that keepeth the law, happy is he" (KJV). It is important for churches to have a vision for mission and that means engaging in the *Missio Dei* for your congregation. Wright says, "we have to start by seeing ourselves within the great flow of God's mission, and we must make sure that our own missional goals – long term and more immediate – are in line with God's."[4] It seems that this is the foundation that many local congregations miss, as they are not seeing themselves as part of the mission and have no vision for mission beyond their four walls.

When there is a vision for mission, this creates a common cause that people can rally around. It gives them something to focus on outside of their internal problems and gives them an opportunity to experience the love and grace of God in action. John Wesley spoke to this issue and said that reaching out to others "cannot be done by proxy,"[5] but requires the personal involvement of the Christian. Whatever form the *Missio Dei* takes in the local church, it must take place and be part of the

---

[4] Wright, 23.

[5] John Wesley, *Sermons on Several Occasions: On Visiting the Sick* (n.p.: Apple Books, 1771), 3594.

foundation. To be part of the *Missio Dei* is to participate in God's plan and purpose and this is a cause that we can all support and rally around.

Conclusion

Looking back, 2020 is one of those years that many of us are thankful to be past. The Corona Virus, that still ravages the world as of the time of my writing, has taught us many things: the fragility of human life, the interconnectedness of our global community, and perhaps also how much our values have become misplaced. The constant rush of the pre-COVID world has given way to a forced change of pace; certain cultural idols have been shaken; the inequalities of our Western society have become more obvious.

Speaking as a student of the Christian church, there have also been many aspects that we, institutionally speaking, have taken for granted, which this virus has brought into question and focus. Should the church be dependant on physical structures or activity-based programing? What is to be the role of social media and the online world? How are we to define "church"? What practices and rituals have we taken for granted, which we find ourselves missing when they are taken away? How do we adapt our rituals and practices to a different context, ie. the online world? What is to be the church's response to government mandates, particularly as it relates to the health and safety of our communities? What even is the church's role in the surrounding community?

This collection of student essays, though not explicitly asking these questions, definitely show that these are some of the queries that come to the foreground, along with certain theological quandaries, such as how to interpret the pandemic in light of God's goodness and sovereignty; the struggle with evil in a good but broken world; and the ironic timing of the shutdowns to the holiday that we all know as Easter – one that Christians point to as central for our faith. This annual holiday reminds us Christians of the fact that our hope is centered on the very real shameful suffering and death of our Lord, Jesus, on the Cross, and then the amazing news of his resurrection – a hope that we may also look forward to on the day when he returns in glory. Yet, how does the church represent this hope in a world that seems devoid of hope, that wrestles with a potentially deadly disease that is both unfamiliar and unknown? It does so by pointing to that greater story: that hope is possible, even after the curse of sin and death has done its very worst. This was one of the reasons why each of the essays – even if the timing of when students studied the churches was much later than the actual holiday itself – focussed specifically on the celebration of Easter 2020 and the weeks following.

Theologically speaking, though representing different denominations, worship styles and relative experiences based on location and level of exposure to the COVID pandemic, the churches surveyed seemed to agree that though God did not cause the pandemic to spread, He allowed it to happen for our good – though many were struggling to imagine what that good will be that may come out of this situation; and that God will see us through it. Whether or not COVID was directly mentioned, themes of perseverance and God's grace in the midst of trials were common themes in the messages given. Another common theme was how much humans crave community and intimate relationships. Congregants mentioned missing one another and desiring the chance to hug one another, or at least meet face to face, once again. Pastors mentioned the increased stress from not being able to visit their members who were isolated or in hospitals. Yet, there was another trend that was interesting: while many of those interviewed expressed longing to return to in-person services, several more expressed a preference for the new online format. Could this be a sign of the way churches will need to adapt in the future, or is this a further sign of hyper-individualism and an indicator of those who may not be as serious about faith? Honestly speaking, I believe this is something that only the passage of time will reveal, though speaking as one who has toyed with the idea of online church before this, I do believe that this is a topic worthy of further exploration.

In addressing the practical questions of ministry, each of the churches analyzed in this study came to recognize the need for adaptability and innovation early on, often utilizing the tools available to them, though limited and difficult to implement at first, to develop means to stay connected with one another and to continue offering ministry to their congregations. In several cases, these methods needed to be adapted and improved upon as time progressed, and most mentioned that these new technological methods have enhanced already existing ministry. Smart phones and social media were used for pre-recorded messages; multi-media was incorporated in the Sunday morning experience; chatrooms, video calls, and forums were introduced. Across the board, the use of social media was seen as a beneficial tool for continued ministry efforts, though many found this inferior to in-person gatherings. Among some churches, this was something completely new; among others, there was an online presence previously, but it was under-utilized before the pandemic. Some churches also featured drive-through communion or outdoor services, similar to a drive-in theatre – something that churches in my Canadian homeland got in trouble with our government for attempting.[1]

Additionally, there was also a level of increased intentionality in doing ministry. Some churches enhanced their outreach or social service efforts to the community around them as a direct result of the needs that became apparent with the evolving situation of the pandemic. Others became more intentional about direct member care, organizing teams to contact at-risk members of the church via telephone on a more regular basis than prior to the pandemic.

However, as Hartlen Coats illustrates in his submission, the shutdown has also led to the death of some churches. The number of churches that will permanently shut their doors as a result of COVID are still unknown. However, as could be seen by the example of the church studied in that chapter, much like many of those people who became terminally ill and died from COVID-related causes, there were also pre-existing conditions in the health of that particular church that led to the final demise of that congregation. Even in the case of those churches that are still functional, disgruntled members (and, one could assume,

1 For specific cases, cf. Austin Grabish "Manitoba church fined $5K for holding service that broke public health order" CBC News November 25, 2020. URL: https://www.cbc.ca/news/canada/manitoba/church-of-god-fined-1.5816259; Brittany Greenslade "Decision on Winnipeg Church's fight for drive-in religious services on hold" *Global News* December 3, 2020. URL: https://globalnews.ca/news/7499519/decision-winnipeg-church-drive-in-religious-services/; Mason DePatie "After $37,000 in fines, court rules Winnipeg church's drive-in service breaches health orders" *CTV NEWS* December 5, 2020. URL: https://winnipeg.ctvnews.ca/after-37-000-in-fines-court-rules-winnipeg-church-s-drive-in-service-breaches-health-orders-1.5218706.

pastors) used the stress of the pandemic and the government-mandated shut-downs to leave their churches to search for fellowship elsewhere.

As my colleague, Dr. Danielson, mentioned in the introduction, my work as a teaching intern was done primarily at a distance, as my family and I made the choice to return to Canada in March because of a televised message from our Prime Minister for all expatriates to return home. In the specific region of Canada we returned to, though there were not many cases of COVID at that time, the government recommendations were followed more strictly there, and because it was a rural area with a less technologically inclined population, many churches shut down completely until restrictions began to be lifted again in the summer. When we chose to return to the United States in August, to continue my studies at Asbury, the situation in that part of Canada was once again gaining a sense of pre-pandemic normalcy, though the officially closed southern border, the constant media coverage, and population control in public spaces was a reminder that the pandemic was still going on. There would also be a later surge of cases in October, forcing another shut-down in that part of the country.

As mentioned by Dr. Danielson, none of us really know what will come in the future. We don't know what the church will look like as it emerges out the other side of this current season. However, a few guesses may be made, based on the findings of this small sampling of churches. For instance, we may not have the same dependency on real estate. We will probably also emphasize more interactivity (as opposed to passive reception), as well as adaptability and tech-savviness. Greater emphasis will be placed on building relationships because of the isolation that the shutdowns have forced upon us. This is in addition to other changes as well that may not have been as obvious in this particular study. Of course, many churches will seek to go back to the former ways of doing things, but even if these changes that COVID has forced us to practice could be implemented into the wider church DNA, I see that as a potentially positive sign.

Greg S. Whyte
PhD Student, Asbury Theological Seminary
Feb. 17, 2021

www.ingramcontent.com/pod-product-compliance
Lightning Source LLC
LaVergne TN
LVHW050627100826
845148LV00011B/1771

* 9 7 8 1 6 4 8 1 7 0 3 5 5 *